Barry Pilton was born in 1946 in Croydon, and educated at Dulwich College and King's College, London. In 1967-8 he lived in Paris and taught English. In 1969 he worked in Fleet Street as a journalist for the *Sunday Post*. Before eventually becoming a freelance writer in 1976 he trained unsuccessfully as a surveyor, a fork-lift truck driver, a furniture removal man, a cooking-oil operative, and a dishwasher; on days off he travelled extensively in Europe, the Middle East, North Africa and the U.S.A. Since 1984 he has lived in mid-Wales.

TV work includes sit-coms *Shelley* and *It Takes a Worried Man*, comedy show *Not The Nine O'Clock News*, and the plays *Everyone A Winner* and *Slimming Down*. Extensive radio work ranges from Radio 3 talks to documentary series, sketch shows and situation comedy. These include *The 27 Year Itch*, *Weekending*, *The Jason Explanation*, *Miles of London*, and *Degrees of Humour*, a history of the Cambridge Footlights. He broadcasts occasionally, was a chatter on the live chat-show *Extra Dry Sherrin*, and has written for *Punch*. He also contributes regularly to *Country Living* and is editor of *The Breconshire Naturalist* (circ. 750 and rising).

Previous books are *One Man and His Bog* and *Miles of London*.

One Man and His Log started life as a Radio 4 series of talks.

also by Barry Pilton

ONE MAN AND HIS BOG

and published by Corgi Books

ONE MAN AND HIS LOG

Barry Pilton

CORGI BOOKS

ONE MAN AND HIS LOG

A CORGI BOOK   0552 13233 0

First publication in Great Britain

PRINTING HISTORY

Corgi edition published 1988

This book is set in 11/12 Times

Corgi Books are published by Transworld Publishers Ltd.,
61-63 Uxbridge Road, Ealing, London W5 5SA, in Australia by
Transworld Publishers (Australia) Pty. Ltd., 15-23 Helles Avenue,
Moorebank, NSW 2170, and in New Zealand by Transworld Publishers
(N.Z.) Ltd., Cnr. Moselle and Waipareira Avenues, Henderson,
Auckland.

Printed and bound in Great Britain by
Hazell Watson & Viney Limited
Member of BPCC plc
Aylesbury, Bucks, England

*This book is dedicated to
the libel lawyers of my
fellow crew-members*

FOREWORD

In the interests of documentary accuracy, I have checked the events described in this book with the other four participants. There was general agreement that we had visited France, and three of the four could remember a boat. However, the name and location of the canal caused some quite heated debate and thereafter the reliability of the others' memories became most questionable. The central importance of my role came under attack, and there was widespread and irrational disagreement over my interpretation of events occurring after 0100 hours on day One. (Indeed the reunion eventually broke up in what I consider quite unnecessary violence.) Unfortunately, the supply of information proved so undisciplined that there now exists a school of thought that we had five separate holidays. Moreover, as a result of my (eminently reasonable) refusal to allow the placing of four separate sets of footnotes on each page — not to mention a series of highly inflammatory appendices — there is now the strong likelihood that by next spring the book market on Burgundy canal holidays will be close to saturation point. It is therefore most advisable to have early access to an authoritative version of events. Mine.

Strange things people say before they've been on a canal barge in France:

May is the ideal month for a French canal barge holiday..

CHAPTER ONE

The couple at the next table were quite clearly from France. This was an assessment based less upon recherché observation of cultural nuance than on their mastery of French — though, admittedly, our belief that they were fluent did spring mainly from an inability to make any sense of their conversation. Nonetheless, even the sound of a *merde* or two is evocative enough for the Francophile to go culturally weak at the knees and wax on about *baguettes* and *boules* and Bardots. And so, as the untranslated repartee of the middle-aged pair flowed on, undercurrents of the French intellectual tradition, of Gallic passion, and of musical Mediterranean sensuality appeared increasingly evident to us. With every fresh *Zut alors!* that surfaced into the dawn air-conditioning of the channel ferry, the exoticism of a foreign culture grew stronger. The aura of the couple's mysterious but definitely superior existence became ever-more alluring — until it was noticed that the cause of their animation was the Bingo section of their French newspaper.

This laudable homage to our EEC allies was also reflected in our choice of a French ferry to chug across the English Channel. Admittedly, the cultural content of a mass transit system is limited but the French have a way with coffee and barmen and decor that makes an ersatz France start at Dover, a floating *hors d'oeuvre* to the holiday proper. Perhaps such a preference is partly snobbism — of a sort that would consider lung cancer to be chic if caused by a Gitane — but, for travellers eager to resume their love affair with France, a lap of the boat's atmospheric innards is like prolonged foreplay. At the very least it avoids boredom, and at sea distractions which keep the mind occupied often prevent the stomach being vacated. The other great perk is the security of knowing the officials are bilingual and French, which enables faint-hearts to play at *la langue française* with a safety net.

As we throbbed out of the harbour, however, some of our thoughts were already aboard another boat — an altogether smaller vessel, half the size of the average wave, with no staff, no duty-free, no cooked breakfasts, and a pair of cabins that no safety-conscious cat would ever allow itself to be swung in. Our holiday barge.

Moored somewhere in the heart of shallowest Burgundy, this off-season dreamboat was, as the forms say, 'purpose of journey'. As a holiday location, it may have only rated 1 on the Ambre Solaire protection scale, and its night-life was probably found less in clubs than ponds, but the *quinze jours* represented (to this crew-member, at any rate) the joyous completion of childhood, albeit twenty years behind schedule, by making real the fantasy of a proper, a working, a larger-than-loofah-size boat to play with; whether it would be possible to re-enact the entire plot of *Swallows and Amazons* within that time scale remained to be seen.

As the rising sun shed cold light on the rising waves,

more bodies and baggage started to slump into the empty seats. In everyday life, this would be an averagely unriveting event, but a side-effect of travel is that all five senses are constantly on red alert, eager to observe, and to listen, and to sniff, (and, if Italian, to grope) in the cause of any new experience. And since, in these days of mass tourism, the only remaining anthropological interest of travel is other travellers, this arrival of fellow ticket-holders inspired prolonged study. No doubt to a novelist the lounge area had enough basic material for a set of Booker prizes, but unfortunately the imagination of the lay observer is prone to somewhat rigid preconceptions. Since the early 1970s, whenever nine or ten people are gathered together in the name of a journey, be it by boat, spaceship or lift, they all somehow bear an uncanny resemblance to the unique social sub-groups of a disaster movie; before the ferry was two miles off the coast we had not only identified the one who would take charge, the one who would crack up, and the one who would have a baby, but had also spotted the escaped convict, the ethnic minority scapegoat, and the carrier of a deadly virus. This did not, as value judgments go, seem a significant breakdown of insular thought-patterns — travel's broadening of the mind presumably only comes after French passport control.

More perhaps to the point, any in-depth study of character and group dynamics among our little band of bargees would also have to await the arrival of France — our earlier midnight rendezvous in a wet, dark inner city was only the second time that all five of us had been together. This, though, is not to imply that we were a group of total strangers, with only a red carnation and a ferry ticket in common; on the contrary, the exact nature of the inter-connecting relationships among myself, Susan, Angus, Arabella and Trixie was worthy of a Logic question in a Tripos paper: 'If each of the five knows at

11

least two people, and three of the five know three people, and one of the five knows four people, what is the maximum number that can be in a cabin at any given time without introductions being necessary?' ('Know', for the purposes of this question, having no carnal overtones.)

Only as we sat there together, semi-taciturn, but senses-a-go-go, and surrounded by foreign paintwork and bilingual intercoms, did it finally sink in that our holiday plans had advanced from 10 per cent deposit to 100 per cent reality, and that henceforth we would be known as 'crew'.

Feeling discreetly sensitive, both to the social complexities of this new role — once likened to group marriage on water — and to any unpredictable behaviour patterns in our new friends, the opening conversational gambits of our holiday took on much of the flair and originality of Pawn to K4. When, therefore, the announcement of an imminent *petit déjeuner* was purred to all passengers (only the French can sound erotic over a public address system), we looked forward to it not just as our first social engagement of the trip but also as an opportunity to move beyond first-name terms and into the business of empathy-building. Being sophisticated, consciousness-raised, middle-class persons, we prepared to exchange cultural CVs and to set about the introduction of psyches.

Unfortunately, the croissants appeared over the horizon at the same time as a Force 8. At first, as we made our way for'ard and food'ard, it was confidently thought — ours being the generation of seasoned voyagers — that the group's appetite and keenness could survive anything, except perhaps the sighting of a dead albatross. One of our number had, however, lived her life in the shelter of the BBC, a vast organisation devoid of natural light, whose employees tend to be stunted and prematurely stained grey. A sudden roll took a sudden toll, and by the time we reached the breakfast table our cutlery requirement was down 20 per cent; while we were downing fruit juices, Susan was receiving upwardly-mobile gastric juices. Consequently, our plans to explore hidden depths were largely eclipsed by discussion of the hidden depths exploring her.

Sea-sickness has modernised its image since those early school-trips of the Sixties — no longer are rows of bodies folded over the rail, like a saucy postcard picture in search of a caption. As ferries have got ever-larger, the classic dash for the side has come to defeat all but Olympic vomiters; nowadays, sadly, the dramatic vision of a heaving sea has been replaced by a bum's eye view of a flushing bowl. No longer, either, the sympathetic arm across the shoulders; instead, morale-boosting comments have to be tapped in Morse through a toilet door.

With all this in mind, and stomach, breakfast became a slightly less upbeat affair, the consumption of food cautiously slow (although some of its components moved around the table quite fast) and the conversation flow much subject to interruption, with Arabella and Trixie having to take turns to deliver regular messages of condolence to the Dames. The mood also took its cue from the time: if early evening now has the happy hour, then early morning can surely claim the dopey hour; a few nautical miles out of port, and out-of-synch body-clocks were causing a brain or two to tick over at less-than-idling speed.

But even the faculties of the deceased could scarcely have failed to detect the arrival, in the buffet, of 'the Englishman abroad'. Admittedly, anyone silhouetted against a foreign backdrop has their national identity tics thrust into sharper focus, but the fortissimo presence of the tweeded but truculent gentleman did much to explain the historic misgivings about Albion. (Sightings of one's countrymen abroad do tend to produce an apologetic unease, vaguely reminiscent of having to explain away one's parents on school-visiting day; when fellow English are bumped into on holiday they are usually best thrice denied before cock-crow.) Apparently alone, distinguishedly-stooped, anguishedly-furrowed, and with hair modelled on the later Lloyd George, his unabashed behaviour strongly suggested he was travelling overseas on a British Council bursary to promote the image of Traditional English Eccentrics.

Unique among customers at the food counter, he was enquiring not about the nature of the yoghurts, nor the freshness of the brioches, but was trying to establish the name of the boatyard in which the ferry had been built.

'Spanish is it, the HULL?' was a question clearly unfamiliar to the young French girl at the check-out, whose translator's course in cuisine had touched little upon the finer points of steel foundries.

'Only I wondered about the CONSTRUCTION method,' was an explanation that, predictably, advanced the conversation little further. There was a brief silence to enable the echoes of his voice to bounce off all four walls. A nervous frisson, this time unrelated to vomit, ran up and down the English-speaking spines present; the *joueurs au Bingo*, also present, were murmuring amongst themselves, probably wondering which central tenets of English economic theory were being discussed, and why.

'You can do anything with STEEL — did you realise that?' he bellowed. She smiled, again, helplessly short of diversionary tactics since, his journey the length of the buffet bar being for intellectual research purposes only, he had with him no tray of contents, and indeed no tray.

'Thought there might have been a PLAQUE. You know, of origin. Like BLUE plaques, on walls. You've not seen one?'

'No, monsieur. Sorry.' She shook her head sadly, no doubt longing for the simple verities of football hooligans.

He turned away from her slowly, considered matters, and then wandered back down the line and out of the door, apparently quite unaware that he had the undivided attention of an entire self-service restaurant.

It was the one small drama of the crossing. Although it only lasted 0.25 of a Continental breakfast, the abiding hope of such journeys is such dramas. Rarely is a larger cross-section of strangers confined together, and yet — like a multi-cultural unmelting pot where the ingredients are seldom stirred and the gas never lit — they mostly travel in suspended animation. In the main (pun intended), passengers behave with the caution of any species in unknown territory, claiming few rights, deferring to peaked caps, and not speaking to strangers; for a few disorienting hours, a ferry almost forms a working model of the UN Charter.

And very quiet it generally was, in the buffet that late May day. Already Arabella was starting to yawn, and Angus had begun to read a large book with an intensity that suggested he had been set homework for the hols. The only real sign of activity, and one which transcended national boundaries, was a tendency to patting. Patting is specifically a traveller's ailment, causing the sufferer to suddenly, nervously, pat key parts of the body; if a bulge is discovered, usually in the shape of a passport or AA 5 Star Insurance, immediate cathartic relief is experienced. This relief lasts, on average, about five minutes; a repeat course of treatment is then required. Among the four of us, however, we had the additional psychological trauma of all the paperwork for two cars, one barge and a return ferry; we regularly emptied our pockets onto the table with a speed which would have silenced even the most unreasonable of Met. policemen.

Such insecurity about our belongings is hard to explain rationally. Naturally, being liberals, we did not subscribe to the view that the international pickpocket density becomes dramatically higher on the far side of the three mile limit; nor did I much like the theory that senile dementia was now widespread among the under-thirties. Rather, the root cause seemed a primeval touch of the Kafkas, a fear that a man without his Green Card is due for an extended candle-lit tour of European dungeons. And, although we gave the problem of document security the benefit of two long, slow *cafés noirs*' worth of thought, our sole solution — to have one's sun, sea, sand and sex in a Securicor Van — was felt to lack the necessary holiday magic. Indeed, the only obvious foolproof system is to secrete any vital items in an orifice as do spies and drug smugglers, but it does seem likely that production of essential travel documents from a rear passage could jeopardise the chances of an harmonious relationship with the authorities.

With Arabella starting to doze, and Angus apparently starting to write notes, Trixie and I sat and sipped in silence — seated, incidentally, on stunningly modern French chairs, which had for some reason been designed to achieve a lower drag co-efficient factor than most Formula One racing cars. And then an unseen management hand — sailors seem a rare commodity in the corporate structure of large car-ferries — plugged in an earful of up-market Muzak, and seamless Mendelssohn began to seep everywhere, as if the ship's doctor had decided to prescribe Valium by air; it was probably in accordance with some passenger evaluation study showing half-a-Channel's width to be the maximum distance that the average holiday-maker can survive silence without psychological trauma.

Although only a few centimetres down our third black coffee, an urge for a ferry walkabout came upon me, an inner restlessness coinciding with an outer calm as the unexpected squalls began to fade. (At least, they *seemed* unexpected — the frequency with which such storms manage to pinpoint holiday ferries does raise a suspicion that their cause may not be deep frontal systems but well-funded lobbyists from the Chunnel construction project.) A further solicitous message was relayed into the ladies' toilets, this time to check whether the personal waters of our missing member were also subsiding, and to ask how many limbs she had available for a stroll. Unfortunately, it appeared that our Susan expected to be there for the duration — if not indeed for the afternoon return journey. And so, with Angus and Arabella otherwise engaged and disengaged, it was just Trixie and I who set off, pausing at the Duty Free to see if it stocked Get Well cards.

Regrettably, the alcohol section of the Duty Free proved to be the outermost limit of Trixie's walking ambitions.

For the truly indefatigable tourist, a solo circumnavigation of a ferry boat, although hardly ranking as a traditional voyage of discovery, always has its rewards. Admittedly to the fatigable tourist, it is an object exercise in objectionable exercise, but this ignores the enthusiast's pleasure in seeking out still-unspoilt corners of the boat, in stumbling across little-known viewpoints and in exploring deserted gangways with only the sound of the engines for company. In part, it is a way of siphoning off excess adrenalin while waiting for the T of ETA to turn up, but also it is an attitude of mind which cannot see even a derelict slag-heap without wanting to investigate. And with all of France soon to investigate, this dummy run at sight-seeing provided just about the only distraction for a gathering nervous excitement.

The holiday was clearly under way. Little more than three official hours of it had so far gone, and yet, with

Susan water-closeted in the rest-room facilities, Arabella comatosely-asleep in the tea-lounge, Angus unavailable for public comment, Trixie vigorously active in the *vin rouge* department, and myself struggling to find a way through to Level 4 of the bilges, the different preferences of the group were already starting to be established.

CHAPTER TWO

The very old Riley led the quite very old Renault in the long haul across Northern France, that inevitable prelude to the dash South; my aim was to keep on going throughout the day, stopping only for tolls and bladders, and reach our Burgundy canal in time to cast off on the late afternoon ripple. The choice of Riley as convoy-leader was on the unflattering grounds that its early, and odds-on, demise would be more easily noticed if it were in front. This proved an unwarranted slur. The car behaved impeccably, if only because it was rarely called upon to exceed fifteen k.p.h. for hours on end, the whole of Artois being rather beautifully gift-wrapped in fog.

The two males drove. This though was no chauvinist chauffeurism. Arabella was a non-driver, thanks to an eyesight that would have made her a liability even as a bat, Susan was still in post-ferry shock, and Trixie had a broken arm. (Although this arm was, with a hint of heroic reticence, alluded to by her as an 'accident of *les pistes*', closer questioning would reveal one of the less

19

glorious episodes in ski-ing history: she had, the previous week, tripped and broken it while walking towards a dry ski-slope somewhere near Telford New Town.) Applications for position of navigator, the traditional role of fall-guy in holiday motoring, were disappointingly few, made fewer by the discovery that our map predated the nationwide renumbering of the French road system. It was, however, initially easy to grasp the correct Continental drift as the familiar cavalcade of Little Englander headlights with the regulation eye-patches and yellow make-up led the way out of port and into open country.

For miles, the passing landscape remained an enigma firmly Sellotaped in a mystery, invisible apart from the roadside trees moving ethereally by at jogging pace, each trunk vanishing upwards into a fuzzy pinkish-grey halo. But the villages and small country towns were instant proof, if proof were needed, that the ferry-driver had hit France spot-on; the inimitable cobbles, the fading pre-war wall advertisements, the unnaturally deserted streets, the occasional sighting of a widow in black, with loaf — even the most theoretically unprepossessing of townscapes looked evocatively like reproductions of the voguish soft-focus *cartes postales*. Such camera-trembling sights made our deadline seem, in a perverse way, almost cause for relief, as an express drive (well, a non-stopping slow drive) through the joys of rural France is a cultural offence which demands mitigating circumstances.

In fact, it was not very long before we made our first unscheduled stop. This was next to a ditch, next to nowhere. It was chosen by Susan as the most convenient spot in which to be car-sick — an event which marked her complete recovery from the condition of being sea-sick. This apparently represented a significant improvement in circumstances, as the main complaint of those throwing up in mid-Channel is the unwillingness of the captain to park his boat. And so, she and I being in the lead car, our subsequent progress — not so much whistle-stop as vomit-stop — began to look as though we were thoughtfully leaving strategic piles of spoor to guide the following Renault through the early morning mist.

Months earlier, when selecting my crew (and here I modestly admit to responsibility for the current expeditionary force, having had the original concept in my own bath; I would also, if pressed, claim seminal input into such matters as the choice of vessel, the choice of location, and the obtaining of the brochure — not to mention the borrowing of the Riley), I had been much attracted to Susan, who, it seemed, belonged to that classic category of the 'pale and interesting'; so far, at least 50 per cent of my character assessment appeared to be stunningly perceptive.

In England, a fairly reliable, even sure-fire, way to obtain privacy is to vomit in public; in France, it is usually the signal for a small interested crowd to gather, followed by a discussion, open to the floor, of possible causes and remedies. (There is about the French a lack of prissiness, a recessive Rabelaisian gene perhaps, which allows them to talk readily, unawkwardly, to beyond-the-pale folk like prostitutes and drunks and down-and-outs — and indeed, as once witnessed, to move easily on without social unease should the person suddenly drop dead.) Hence, while *we* were all forming a roadside huddle at a discreet distance from the sound of barfing, a passing peasant *au vélo* — his clothes and appearance corresponding exactly to the sort of ethnic caricature that would have him banned from educational textbooks in England — stopped, and asked interestedly, '*Elle est malade, non*?', and then went across to make further diagnostic enquiries face to face. Anticipation of a traditional herbal remedy deep in his blouson was soon dispelled, as he provided several non-homeopathic pats on the back — tending to

21

the arse region — reminisced briefly about wartime camaraderie, and then extended a formal invitation to inspect his wife and farm. It was human contact of a high order. By comparison, we appeared to be enforcing a quarantine order. Admittedly, keeping our distance was not entirely an over-fastidious reserve — a number of crew-members had prematurely adjusted their dress in readiness for sunny Burgundy, and in consequence found great personal difficulty in standing calf-deep in cold wet grass. (Angus, a bespectacled figure who took his pleasures seriously, was particularly regretting his choice of thonged sandals.) Nonetheless, although barely thirty miles from the coast, our behaviour already made us feel somehow repressedly English — all the more so as we felt obliged to decline his invitation. We regretfully had to explain that time waits for no man, least of all holiday-makers, and our convoy moved on once more. Even by refusing to recognise internationally-agreed French time zones, we and my schedule were steadily parting company.

As the morning wore on, and the mist wore off, the first holiday views of France to be unveiled were, somewhat inauspiciously, of vast cemeteries: the military cemeteries of World War I. It did, though, seem fitting — our minds had already been on death for some time as, ever since embarkation, we had found ourselves overtaken by locals at a speed which suggested that, whatever Larousse may say, there is no word for fog in the French language. Glib comparison is often made between war and the carnage on roads, but if, for road-safety propaganda, the French were to introduce motorist-only cemeteries, it seems likely they would soon cover all the unconsecrated ground still left in Northern France. (And to cater for the French need for *la gloire*, their Ministry of Transport would then also have to erect a Cenotaph to the Unknown Driver around which all the traffic of relatives would probably circle enthusiastically once a year, hooting constantly for two minutes.)

We made our first pit-stop just short of the *auto-route* to Paris. While here, it was felt that both cars could benefit from a change of personnel, and Arabella and Susan swapped places; Trixie being the Renault's owner, she felt (according to Arabella) a captain's duty to stay aboard, as there was apparently a certain disagreement in progress as to the correct use of the clutch . . . and the brake, the accelerator, the steering wheel, the headlights, the indicators and indeed the highway code. For her part, Arabella (claiming to be uninfluenced by this minor civil war) said she felt the time had now come for her to assist in the Riley's navigation — with over a hundred straight miles of motorway ahead she was experiencing a growing confidence that route-finding could well be within her grasp. And meanwhile Susan was persuaded, by me, that her allergy to the internal combustion engine might benefit from a change of suspension.

Indeed, our time at the little village garage was full of incident. While innocently buying some hard-boiled sweets off the mademoiselle in charge, Angus and I came across a rack of pornography so hard-core that in London the Vice Squad would have burst through the door with a set of sledgehammers. Admittedly, in England one is used to petrol stations selling such an extraordinarily wide range of bric-à-brac that one half-expects them to have forgotten to stock the petrol, but a garage had never before seemed a likely outlet for sexual outlets. The sale of such material, however, did much to explain French driving habits, for as a result of encouraging this self-indulgence while on the move a very high proportion of their motorists have clearly gone blind.

There was another surprise to come. As we went to exit from the garage, the Renault 4 gave a couple of gassy belches . . . and hiccuped to a halt. The rest was silence.

Anyone who gums a GB sticker to their boot does so with a keen historical awareness that their journey is remarkably likely to form part of that great oral tradition of stories about 'vehicles that break down on holiday'; a dinner-party of eight can be sustained for the entire evening by such anecdotes, each account trumping the last, until the family who transported their yak-damaged Range Rover back across the Himalayas in twenty-five separate rucksacks are declared the winners. Looked at from the car's point of view, all these breakdowns are eminently reasonable. Humans abroad find it common-place to suffer gippy tummy, so cars must surely therefore be expected to suffer gippy engines — we are often advised not to drink the water, they probably have similar reservations about the petrol. But none of this sociological analysis was of great help in restarting the Renault.

Nor were we. And there followed a few brief moments in which only a 13-digit emergency phone number stood between us and a demonstration of the fragility of civilization. Angus and I at once launched ourselves into the traditional 'lifting of the bonnet' routine, but it rapidly became clear that, in our case, this was a ceremonial event and for purposes of forecourt status only. And then several of us tried to suggest various parts of the engine that might be looked at, but when pressed on 'why' or 'how' or even 'where', it grew noticeable that our knowledge of such items as a carburettor was essentially limited to their spelling. And after even the manual had defeated us, and we had admitted that our combined skills could not tell a death-rattle from a loose screw, there was the sort of sinking feeling we had thought more likely to receive on the barge.

It was Trixie who eventually resolved the crisis. Scorning our late 20th century hi-tech approach, she proposed the old peasant remedy of a pat on the rump.

And, one concerted rump-pat later, we were indeed off once more. It was, though, fortunate we were off for a holiday by boat since the Renault apparently so enjoyed the physical contact that, until back in England, she never again responded to the turn of a key.

Where Susan was pale, Arabella was pink, where Susan was slim, Arabella was rounded, and where Susan was quiet, Arabella was noisy. It was the noise of sudden enthusiasms; Arabella was a great collector of lost causes and lame ducks — indeed her very enthusiasm for the holiday made it suspect! — and in a less emancipated era she would have been the beribboned holder of the King's Award for services to bring-and-buy sales. An improbable solicitor, radical except for her vowel sounds and taste in necklaces, her conversation was constantly sprinkled with impromptu judgments, few of which stood up on appeal. Selection of Angus and Arabella for the trip (being intermittently devoted to each other, they came as a job-lot) had had to rely on my knowledge of old — albeit knowledge of old dinner parties rather than of 14-day boat cruises; they also had the additional attraction, unique among close friends asked, of being available.

Tapes playing, and all internal organs having resumed normal service, the miles and kilometres at last swept fluently past, as per my holiday blueprint. Continental motorways have a quite different design to English ones, and often use two or more lanes; Europe has, apparently, not got a red traffic-cone industry to maintain and it is often possible to drive in top gear for miles.

But as the motorway signs for Paris grew larger — at least to my eyes; Arabella had contact lenses seemingly made from corrugated perspex — the thickening traffic grew faster and rougher, like a river approaching rapids. The treacherous North Face of the *Périphérique* loomed, the most feared of the great ring-roads. (The golden rule for drivers in France is never to enter a large town; French urban expansion is primarily caused by drivers who, being unable to find, let alone follow, the unique municipal system of Exit signs (*Autres Directions* apparently being the French for Circular Tour), are then forced to sell their car and buy a house instead.) For us the way to freedom was to locate and then − other drivers willing − turn on to the A6 South, a road which unfortunately, when off the map in real life, not only uses an alias, *l'Autoroute du Soleil*, but for long periods goes around completely incognito. Equally disconcertingly, it was a search which had to be carried out at twice the speed of braking on a ring-road that was quite unfamiliar with the Queensberry Rules of the North Circular; to steer as well as navigate needed eyes in every bumper.

'The hemlines seem shorter. Look!' Arabella pointed.

It is a common feature of non-drivers to be oblivious to the imminent loss of a No-Claims Bonus; I gave the minimum acceptable response.

'Oh, *crêpes!* Can we stop?'

'Have a boiled sweet.' Signs, and drivers making them, continued to rush by.

'Do we need the map any more?'

'The A6. We still need the A6.'

She rustled the map again, but said little. And then, whilst we were in mid-maelstrom, and I was urgently performing every known manoeuvre short of an entrechat, she provided her conclusions on the motor-car (not, that is, the Riley, but the history of the automotive industry since approx. AD 1900).

'I would never have a car of my own.'

'No?'

'No. It's anti-social. They do far too much damage to the environment.'

'Really?'

Moving in convoy is never easy, as those on the

North Atlantic run found out, but moving in convoy in Paris, where every second driver apparently fancies himself as a U-boat captain, is next to impossible, and poor Angus kept vanishing time and again from my rear-view mirror — only to reappear somewhere unexpected with the haunted look of a Keystone Cop who has just missed six lamp-posts, a tram, and an oncoming train.

'Yes, acid rain, lead poisoning, great chunks carved out of the countryside, I think cars are immoral.'

'Useful, though.' I tried to impart irony.

'So? What's "useful"?'

I had in mind a journey from South London to Burgundy, but before I could speak she gave a resounding cry of 'There!'

Coming up fast was a very large, very busy and typically anonymous junction which, in an ideal world, would have provided pilotage. 'To the right!' came the command. We managed to embed ourselves in the correct mêlée of traffic and Angus, driving as if in a wheeled magnet, managed magnificently to follow us. 'And now it's straight ahead, Burgundy, all the way!' came the tones of ringing confidence.

It was the tones of ringing confidence that should have made me doubtful. It is the first requirement of a lawyer to make a hopeless case sound convincing, and long practice had made Arabella sound almost constantly convincing; indeed the most reliable sign of her wrongness was usually her confidence. In this case, it remained quite undiminished until the very last vestiges of the alleged *Autoroute du Soleil* had fully vanished into the featureless sands of the suburbs. Confirmation of a navigational error — if confirmation were indeed needed — came from the total absence of any other cars going South . . . apart from a following English Renault breaking the city ordinance against the use of car-horns.

27

Here we made the second mistake. Arabella, acting on some deep ancestral instinct which had enabled her forebears to cross trackless seas and deserts by the stars alone, rejected the defeatism of a U-turn and instead advocated a simple, apparently very obvious, trans-suburban short-cut to take us on to the real McCoy A6. Loath to stop the Riley to be force-fed humble-pie by the trio behind us, I abruptly turned East as instructed and, with the Renault still in hot — and bothered and bewildered — pursuit, plunged the car into an arrondissement of Paris never previously touched by tourism. And here we made the next twenty-seven mistakes. Whereas Haussmann designed central Paris along the lines of a grid system, twentieth century city planners have laid out the suburbs more in accordance with an intestinal system, and for every *rue* we roared up, there was an unequal and opposite *rue* which we found ourselves roaring back down. I revved around in S-bends and cul-de-sacs, my blood pressure warning-light flashing on and off, only to become ever more enmeshed in a maze of maisonettes. And as disorientation started to penetrate every fold of our map, definite signs of a temper tantrum began to enter my cornering. On board the pursuing Renault the three victims of this extra-curricular mystery tour wore looks of utter bafflement, mixed frequently with extreme agitation (and, in the case of one of them, extreme motion discomfort), all of which I defiantly ignored. Indeed, as the two speeding cars moved on into a little-publicised industrial sector, and Arabella's remaining hunches about the A6 faded into a diplomatic right of silence, the only thought on my mind was Cliff Richard, as, through clenched lips, I found myself determinedly, repeatedly, humming out the words 'We're all going on a Summer Holiday . . .'. And then, with one final wrong turn too many, we passed through a pair of large iron gates and both cars came at last, savagely, to a halt . . . in the loading bay of an abattoir.

CHAPTER THREE

Early evening was edging out late afternoon when we drove through the old market town of Corbigny and along the final diminishing mile of lane, track and towpath. It was the hour when the air slips from warm to balmy, and I was navigating the ruts with one arm languidly, if unaerodynamically, held up to the breeze when I saw *Beaujolais Deux*, our barge-to-be, for the first time. Raising my hand in the manner favoured by every cavalry commander since John Wayne, I brought the convoy to a halt on a little bridge crossing the canal. Everyone dismounted, and we all leaned over its brick parapet, scattering the last of the lounging lizards, to look down at the boatyard that awaited us.

'Boatyard' was the hyperbole of the brochure. Instead of our expectation of Burgundian Upper Clyde (the busy Clyde of folkloric memory, that is), there were a couple of old houseboats, for staff, a wooden shed, for the transacting of money, and a clearing in the trees, for parking; come September, the boats would slip their leash, the hut would go back in its Lego box, the clearing would be made fit for weeds again — and the holiday industry would retrench and vanish like thieves in the night. The setting for this shoestring outpost of tourism was what the brochure would doubtless call a 'lagoon', a stretch of canal widened to international football-pitch size for some long-forgotten industrial purpose, hinted at by an occasional derelict building hidden in the trees and the odd overgrown quarry hidden in the brambles.

We gently freewheeled down the final metres to the moorings, savouring our (late) arrival. Although Saturday was billed as arrivals and departures day, the only sense of hustle and bustle came from the back legs of crickets. In the clearing stood a handful of empty cars (five GB and one D — testimony to the unwritten tourist law that no foreign holiday location is ever without a statutory German); and on the water stood, presumably, a handful of empty spaces. Only a couple of brochure boats were . . . well, the temptation is to say 'bobbing up and down', but canalwater is a rigorous tester of aquatic clichés, since, if left alone, it usually declines to move at all.

'Given you up!'

A bronzed male figure in shorts, and the sort of legs that should be more widely supplied with shorts, emerged from one of the houseboats; a middle-aged beard gave him an effective hint of laid-back ruggedness. '*Périphérique*, was it?'

Our barge was the outer vessel of the pair remaining, and, with that minimum of formality appropriate to half-naked officials, he beckoned us to follow him across the intervening boat. As we did so, we made an effort to staunch our last-lap adrenalin, aware somehow that to leap about crying 'Whoopee!' might not be thought a very adult response to the sight of a thirty-nine foot canal boat. Instead, conscious also that on deck he showed an agility suggestive of magnetic espadrilles, we all concentrated extremely hard on proving we had qualified sea-legs, and managed to restrict the number who fell over cleats to two.

We were taken on a brief, preliminary inspection, the hire-boat equivalent of feeling the hotel mattress — though here the analogy seems to peter out, as the likelihood of anyone saying 'No, thanks. Not what we expected' and going back home, is presumably confined to employees of the Consumers' Association. Indeed, the single observation of substance that our group made about the boat was 'Oh, it's blue and white!' Our presence aboard seemed, to me at least, a dream come true, and I found myself roaming the deck, surreptitiously stroking the ropes and wobbling the wheel and fiddling with fenders. Several times I rippled the water with my fingers, as though testing its suitability for a boat. In part, this was the hyperactivity of frustration — my mind was already running an Agfacolour home-movie of all the *scènes rustiques* which would have to wait another day. North from the lagoon, the Canal du Nivernais initially takes an unbending course, flowing straight as a wet arrow, and the sight of the awaiting nautical miles only added to my impatience. But the sun had moved another notch lower and still ahead of us lay the unloading of the car, the loading of the boat, the unloading of our wallets, the loading of his; a crash course in boat mechanics, a non-crash course in steering; and the testing, selection and hiring of miniature bicycles. A night in the blackish lagoon loomed.

I sighed, and mentally stuck a pin in a model of the French Minister of Transport. Out in the lagoon, the one remaining family still working on their mastery of steering in a circle uncertainly straightened up their *Beaujolais Trois* and, to the sound of giggles, made a tentative but 75 per cent successful departure into the canal proper. Their boat-horn gave a series of blasts new to maritime law and several unidentified arms waved a cheery goodbye. Across the water the strained voice of their captain was heard calling out, 'No, you can't have the fish fingers yet!' and with that another English family holiday was under way. The sun meanwhile had slipped a further notch.

'Don't worry! We'll get you away today!' Our grizzled English rep sucked at an authentically marine-looking pipe and smiled reassuringly.

Those few nectarine words provided the joyous culmination not only to my months of planning, but to years of unfulfilled longing.

Inspired as a child by Mr J. Masefield's request for a tall ship and a star to steer her by, but less enamoured, as an adult, by the concept of water with bumps on, I had therefore settled long ago on a miniaturised ambition for a narrow boat and a bank to steer her by, and from every winter's travel pages since had carefully pruned the barges' section. This winter, finally, I had advanced to catalogues and small print, and so had weighed Llangollen Viaduct against the Canal du Midi, made cost analyses of companies and comparative studies of climates, formed aesthetic judgments on classes of boats, and generally gained a slight intellectual edge should buoyancy aids and bilge pumps ever figure in a conversation. Today the choosing was over; I had absorbed all the bumf on Burgundy, made myself fully *au fait* with Mr Michelin, and my blue tourist touch-paper was ready for lighting — ahead lay kingfishers and red squirrels, châteaux and 12th century churches, rivers and forests, and all the local peasants that the Tourist Board could muster.

'Oh, let's stay here tonight. I saw a couple of good bars in town.'

I eyed Trixie's unbroken arm. 'Pardon?'

'Need a good piss-up after today!'

'Just three miles down and we can moor by a chateau.'

'What I want most is a wash and a chit-o!'

Whereas selection of Arabella and Angus had relied on knowledge of old, selection of Trixie had relied on knowledge of Angus. 'University drinking pals' he had said, with what I had taken to be colloquial rhetoric. Requests for a character reference had produced encouraging mention of liveliness; this liveliness now seemed to have unexpectedly robust qualities. A largish, spiky-haired woman, she had a jaw that jutted and a pair of eyes that took no prisoners. I paused, to choose an ally.

Arabella, who rarely pauses, said, 'And we must do a big shop.' Arabella had been raised in her family hotel and, the art of victualling now inbred, never found herself able to visit even a friend's bedsit without compulsively filling it with the contents of a supermarket. She said no more, and I knew from her detached look that she was compiling a shopping list for five persons for two weeks – plus essential extras for unexpected guests and coach parties.

If we were to cast off tonight, I now needed strong backing. I ruled out Susan. She was the only one of us who, during the inspection, had indeed felt the mattresses, clearly being of the view that arrival would best be celebrated by doing something comatose; she also preferred to win arguments by the long, erosive process of silence, and time was short. I considered Angus. His position was hard to fathom – indeed most, if not all, of his positions were hard to fathom. He had a degree in philosophy, an interesting collection of abstract concepts, and regularly lost sleep over the meaning of life. Had he a 'Who's Who' entry, he would, under hobbies, have put 'The Theory of Knowledge'.

'Expect you want to get a move on?' I enquired hopefully of him. Part of my tentativeness seemed born of a peculiar fear that Arabella would accuse me of leading my witness, and disqualify the question.

'Er, well . . . I would like to unpack my books first. Sort them out.'

'And card-index them?' were the words on my tongue, but they went unused — I had recognised defeat. And, as I knew how many books he had brought (to the approximate kilo, at least), I also wanted to avoid the possibility of his adopting the suggestion.

'Well,' said our boat adviser, 'I'll leave you to it then,' and returned with prehensile aplomb to the bank. 'Give us a shout if you want me.' I sensed he was disappointed in us.

To my perverse satisfaction, the group found it no easier to organise themselves for the night-spots and leading delicatessens of Corbigny than I had found it to organise them into a crack holiday-making squad. A recurring difficulty was the meaning of the simple word 'ready', which unexpectedly lent itself to sufficient interpretations to occupy a team of theologians. Some wanted to fully unpack, some supported the half-unpack option, and others were content to loosen a zip; there was no agreed norm on ablution time, with some favouring the quick flannel flick, and others the in-depth orifice approach; and while one faction argued that the remaining bread, apples and boiled sweets be mixed into a quick, if unusual, snack, another lobby advanced the nutritional case for delay and a blow-out *français*. In addition, the luggage itself proved a particular stumbling-block, since the ratio of luggage to luggage-space appeared to break all known records, coming in at 6:1.

At least, though, the allocation of cabins was trouble-free; among Angus's intellectual achievements was a Ph.D. in housing management, and we had all been keen to avoid the need for his disputes procedure, lest we were awarded accommodation by a points system based on

Angus-worship and bribery. He and Arabella took the double-berthed cabin for'ard (known by day as the galley), Susan and I took the double-berthed cabin aft, and Trixie took the twin-berthed cabin in between. It was the vacant bed that was the blot on my blue-print (indeed, as a result of my abortive attempt to fill just three double cabins I had come to regard the achievement of Noah in a completely new light); Trixie had initially been signed on as a couple, but the breaking of her arm, with its consequent reduction of amatory positions, had also severed her affair — suggesting a love that was only bone-deep. (Her job was the restoration of Old Masters; her hobby, she said, was invigoration by young masters.) With our complement cut from 6 to 4½, much reliance had been placed on her self-proclaimed ability to obtain a replacement lover, although, being by then plaster-casted, it was uncertain whether she was in pursuit of Platonists or fetishists. And her enthusiasm for the bars suggested the hunt might not yet be over.

When, eventually, we were all ready, over 36 sleepless hours were stacked up behind us, and the only unemptied bags were under our eyes; as we turned and started back to town, it was not just the light which was fading. Fortunately for the unexorcised tourist urge within me, Corbigny's attributes had not caught Mr Michelin's eye, nor turned any Blue Guide prose purple, and I felt excused from sight-seeing duties. Yet it seemed a lovely old stone town, crumbling away in the French tradition (rather than being bulldozed away in the English tradition), and its official insignificance promised well for its more celebrated neighbours. And in the end it did not go altogether unseen as we were led by Arabella on a comprehensive circuit of cheese, veg, *viande* and *vin* shops; this was, however, less a tribute to her thoroughness than a result of their all being closed. A lesser shopper would have rung up No Sale and given in, but her victualling instincts proved very sound — food is so important to the French that one almost expects groceries to be obtainable by a 999 call — and she triumphantly tracked down the one cornerstore still open. To avoid witnessing the havoc to our finances — back home, her shopping technique was once likened to a Viking raiding-party with credit cards — I wandered off to look round Corbigny's one recommended church, described cryptically as 'flamboyant Gothic', but unfortunately religion keeps shorter hours than commerce and its doors were firmly shut. By the time I returned from soaking up the French evening smells, the Riley had a bootful and the passengers, it seemed, each had a bellyful.

We by now all shared Trixie's need to end our longest day with a drink. And also, after all the miles in an enclosed car, and all the hours in a colonial boatyard, we very much fancied the long-awaited cultural immersion. The choice of bars seemed essentially a choice of fruit machines, so we picked one at random, ordered a number of spirits with exotic French names — probably only ever drunk by foreigners on holiday — and waited for something indigenous to happen. We did not have to wait long before contact with locals was made.

Chabrol having made us familiar with the social structure of small French towns, we were well prepared for the protocol and the proprieties (and probable discussion of the latest dead bodies) and with this in mind were busy trying to dredge a little basic syntax up from our memory banks. It was, however, not the bourgeoisie but a group of young artisans who acknowledged our presence, and their opening remarks, *'Qu'est-ce que c'est qui pue ici ce soir?' 'Ah, ça doit être des étrangers!'* ('What is it that stinks around here tonight?' 'Oh, that must be foreigners!'), besides suggesting that *entente cordiale* was still a policy subject to local reservations, also raised the possibility we might have embarked on more vigorous an 'activity holiday' than intended. We agreed, therefore, almost unanimously, to ignore the remarks, an easy decision if only because they raised topics whose vocabulary had never been covered by school text-books. Instead, we attempted to chat on, *entre nous*, and would have buried our noses in our drinks had it not been for the inconvenient shape of liqueur glasses. Their response was a running commentary, and running laughter, on us and what appeared to be obscure personal matters such as breast sizes. By our second round of drinks, though, the bovver-*garçons*, concerned lest we might be having translation difficulties (and we were), had started to provide animal noise sub-titles, mostly pig. And so, although Trixie, the dissenting voice to our silence, and the largest-breasted, had certain international signs which she wished to introduce into the conversation, it was decided that our first day's holiday had probably run its full course of pleasure, and we withdrew. As we drove back to the boat and the blackish lagoon, I felt a deep longing for the second day.

CHAPTER FOUR

It was a disturbed night. Although the body was knack-
ered, the brain was still going strong, and in the resulting
metabolic confusion my body-clock's alarm continually
went off at odd hours. For a record-breaking second day
I saw the dawn, though this time the haze was internal.
Eager to share the experience, I had tried to interest
Susan.

'What is it?'

'The dawn.'

'Where?'

As it became clear I was just an inexplicable bit-part
in some dream, I left her talking on auto-pilot and went
up on the dewy deck alone. Some early cloud was draping
itself pinkishly across the sun, a few early fish were
plopping up to check the isobars, and I knew instinctively
— deep in the sailor's heart that was beating beneath my
silk dressing-gown — that now was the quintessential
anchor-weighing moment. (Discovery of the boat's
absence of an anchor was to be part of that day's

extremely sharp learning curve.) But, with half the dawn chorus still having an early morning mouth-wash, I also knew instinctively that right now I could only muster sufficient crew for a single-seater kayak. I resigned myself to toss fitfully a little longer and, returning below, I set my sights and my digital bleeper on the more civilized breakfast hour of nine.

At the more civilized breakfast hour of nine, the degree of activity was indistinguishable from that at dawn. By ten, the only change I could detect was that the decibel count from Angus's snoring had dropped to within legal limits. By eleven, I had begun to suspect that I had somehow woken up in a different time zone to the others. By 11.05, my holiday mood had reached fever-pitch and I cracked.

My childhood had been full of Sundays in which the time required to get three generations of Piltons and a Ford Prefect washed, dressed and in working order for a trip to the seaside had considerably exceeded the daylight hours available. So I knew that firm leadership was called for.

The for'ard bedroom did not just double as the galley, it was the sole dining-room, it was the sole lounge, it contained the one and only table and it was also home to the steering-wheel — in grandiloquent brochurese it was 'The Stateroom', but in reality it was the central strategic command area. And it had to be conquered.

I breezed in. 'Morning! Sunny side up?' (The advantage of fried eggs was that they sizzle, and the advantage of a frying pan was that it clunks.) 'Er . . .' (There was a brief moment of confusion while the phrase was thought to be a sexual allusion to the position in which I had discovered them.) 'Yes . . . er, lovely . . . thanks.' And I began preparation of the noisiest half-dozen eggs ever overdone in Central France.

The sub-text of the eggs was not immediately grasped

by Arabella who arranged the pillows around her in a way that would not have disgraced Cleopatra and prepared herself for breakfast in bed — with a permanence that suggested an expectation of lunch, tea and dinner to follow. But the arrival of a hungry Trixie and Susan ended her hopes as the fold-up bed and the fold-down table were mutually exclusive. And, as a result, by the time we sat down for the curiously Anglo-Continental breakfast I had hybridized there were indeed five at least partially-dressed customers up and waiting.

This was clearly the moment to outline the itinerary which I had prepared for the coming fortnight, and to be generally galvanic.

'I thought we'd go as far as Auxerre—'

'—O — where?'

'It's a cathedral city, on the river section, set in the heart of the vineyards, and . . .'

The sleepless bits of my night had been spent in such detailed study of Tourist Lit. that I could by now have chosen the ancient Canal du Nivernais as my special subject for Mastermind. By the time coffee was due, I was moving into full propagandising swing about my plans, and had, I felt, successfully conveyed the need for our group life-style to be a touch more turbo-charged, when Arabella unexpectedly raised the question of black pepper (ground). It was not a shortage that I had previously much noticed, and the enquiry's significance initially escaped me.

'Can't we dye the salt?' I was never a food faddist.

A familiar abstracted look came into her eyes. 'I'll add it to the list for this afternoon then.'

I paused, very nervously, trying to decide whether it would be safer to ask about 'the list' or 'this afternoon'. 'What list?'

'Spice list. We've not got any spices yet.'

From deep within, I suddenly felt 24 hours' worth of

irritation making its way very fast to the surface as I saw before me the surreal prospect of our barge remaining stationary for the next 14 days whilst the aggregating food stocks of Corbigny gradually sank it lower and lower in the water until the packed gunwales slipped from sight and the world's largest private boat collection of groceries went to the canal bottom. We had in the making a poor man's 20th century Quinquireme of Nineveh: 'full of metal tins and plastic cans and going nowhere'.

'Oh I don't think we need any spices just now.'

The unexpectedness of Susan's intervention was almost decisive; her motivation was admittedly mysterious — it was two days before we fully appreciated that rich foreign food was, for her, a season ticket to the nearest toilet — but her opinion was that of an independent. Regrettably, her contribution was marginally preceded by my more forceful proposal that the spices could go screw themselves.

Whereupon Arabella stated that cuisine was a central feature of the holiday, and I stated that perhaps we should have hired a boat in dry dock, and she responded that the surroundings were quite pleasant enough to stay on for another day, and I responded that with eyesight limited to ten feet she was not in a position to judge, whereupon she expressed a critique on the sophistication of my palate, and I expressed a prejudicial assessment of her sensitivity to foreign culture — and then we each paused for breath.

During this brief window of opportunity, Angus, with the benefit of his high IQ, came up with the brilliant proposal that we buy all further provisions *en route*. Whilst this was being digested, I — with a view to forming a Barry-Trixie axis in the shifting alliances — slipped in mention of a rosetted restaurant, some dozen canal miles distant, where excessive alcohol and indeed all known condiments were ready and waiting every night

42

for tired mariners who had read the correct gourmet guides.

Arabella was outflanked, and proposals for cast-off had lift-off. Finally, well after noon, we set about completing the necessary formalities. And most necessary of the formalities was achieving an au faitness with the boat.

By now, however, we were an instructor short; after giving him several of his recommended 'shouts' we found he and his family had embarked upon English Sunday lunch, a meal designed to link up with French Sunday dinner, which in turn forecloses *le weekend*. His Number Two was delegated to us.

Number Two, a younger Englishman in his twenties, was bronzed beyond his years, and clearly fancied himself as a sort of inland beach-bum. He had remarkably large hands, misproportionately so, and an arbitrary collection of muscles that suggested he had enrolled on a Charles Atlas course but had been unable to keep up the payments. He also had hair which grew to excess in unexpected places, but the macho effect seemed limited as they were the kind of places usually favoured by werewolf movies. (This assessment was compiled retrospectively later that night when we were still smarting from the psychological blows inflicted by his barely-disguised disdain of our pallid urban existences.)

If he had been a seaside stick of rock, his body language implied, the words 'Born Free' would have been found at every suck, whereas we, the wretched nine-to-fivers of this earth, had 'Package Tourist' stamped all over our unenterprising pink bodies. And since the chance to shine as lively, interesting human beings never arose during our introduction to pump-action toilets and bilge-emptying, our public image stayed stuck at the far end of the Wimp Scale. Nor did our debuts at the helm help.

People new to steering a boat are always worth a cheap laugh, and we could have filled a music-hall.

It had always seemed a reasonable assumption that, since four m.p.h. is no more than the traditional speed of a well-maintained pedestrian — and one at which he or she successfully avoids brick walls or any other loose pedestrians — then so, too, would four m.p.h. in a motorised boat, in a straight line, in a flat calm, in perfect visibility, be free from any of the incidents which had dogged the *Titanic* and the *Mary Rose*. This proved incorrect. One by one we demonstrated that the shortest distance between two points is, contrary to rumours put about by O Level Geometry, an erratic parabola. Indeed, Arabella's version of a straight line included several 3-point turns. After ten minutes' tuition in 'steady ahead' we had left a wake which resembled the efforts of an infant school's creative drawing class.

'Well, that should shake off any enemy submarines,' was Number Two's sole comment. His machismo had become tangible enough to be patented.

Gradually we grasped the first law of boating: to every action, there is an unequal and inapposite reaction. But the absence of power-steering and anti-lock brakes still remained a constant surprise.

So many months of angst and controversy had preceded my eventual choice of craft that an outsider might reasonably have expected to find her surrounded by America's Cup security guards and wrapped in a large brown paper bag. However, my abiding concern had, perhaps unfortunately, not been with high-speed cornering and aerodynamic toilet facilities, but with social image. There is a certain class of vessel — the neutered speedboat, the midget cruiser, with even their wakes in poor taste — which is much favoured by the type of men who dangle half a hundredweight of gold medallions over half an acre of chest hair, and for whom the highest nautical ambition is to own a monogrammed anchor. I, on the other hand, have always favoured 'the narrow boat', the tasteful, traditional, artisan craft that ensures an historical oneness with the rural scene. (Admittedly, the authenticity of *Beaujolais Deux* was not total; dating, as she did, from circa 1979, the boat provided — and I quote the brochure — not just a State Room, but a Sun Deck and a Flying Bridge Steering Position, none of which seemed very likely features of 19th century barge life.) To glide elegiacally through pastoral settings, the engine's chords throbbing mutedly in time with the cicadas, had always been the leitmotif of my holiday plans.

After Trixie had zigzagged to and fro for five action-packed minutes, spinning the wheel with her unplastered arm and thrusting at the throttle-control with her groin, our induction was declared complete. The relevant factor, according to Number Two, was not that we were proficient but that we were insured.

We went back to the canal bank for one last time, for bicycles and paperwork. Five minutes of rummaging through the large stockpile of miniature bicycles soon showed that little concession had been made for the variable buttock sizes of our party, or indeed for fashion and colour co-ordination, and so we restricted ourselves to choosing models that had a wheel at each end and brakes. Then we completed the little light admin. that remained (essentially a euphemism for the transfer of a crisp travellers' cheque); we made a large asterisked note of emergency telephone numbers; and we thrust our pink baby-smooth hands into the giant calloused maulers of Number Two, and said adieu.

We were about to cast off when Angus, ever the pedant, raised a question of detail which had been troubling him.

' "Knots"?' said Number Two.

'To tie the boat up with.'

'Oh, don't worry,' he said dismissively. 'It's all in your book. About page 15, I think.'

Angus looked as if he was about to worry. I intervened, lest he made a request for evening classes. 'Come along!' I breezed, trying not to sound like a tour-guide. 'Time to set off for Auxerre!' and just restrained myself from adding 'the beautiful cathedral city'. Though I did hear myself lapse into an encouraging 'And we don't want to miss that little candle-lit bistro!'

And the five of us, and four bicycles, took a last look round, cast off the ropes, signalled right, and, some 24 hours late, *Beaujolais Deux* finally chugged away from the bank.

Three unexpected events then happened in quick succession.

It began to rain, in drops twice the size of a five franc piece; a dispute about captaincy broke out the length and breadth of the boat . . . and *Beaujolais Deux* rammed the opposite bank.

CHAPTER FIVE

I would like to make it quite clear that I had no interest in the position of captain for any purpose of personal aggrandisement. I simply felt that, as the initiator of the holiday, the planner, the organiser, the guide, the ideas-man — and the only person who had read page 15, let alone the rest of the handbook — I could possibly be of service to the other crew-members. I also feared that, under more lax leadership, Arabella would never get out of bed, nor Angus out of a book, Trixie out of a gin bottle, or Susan out of the toilet — or indeed the boat out of her berth. Certainly, the need to average thirteen miles per day could easily cease to be a manifesto commitment. At least under my captaincy I could make the canals run on time. Aware that excess lobbying can be counter-productive, I awaited my chance to emerge more or less naturally as the man of the hour. Around the second minute I sensed an opportunity. We were all on deck, trying to contribute to a barnstorming session on possible ways of coiling a rope; at the same time, Angus was conducting experiments with reverse engine thrust, Susan was uncertainly raising and lowering fenders, as if taking the temperature of the canal, and Trixie was trying to drag the sun-beds to a position that would catch the weakening sun. A model of languid disinterest, I spoke.

'I guess we'd better choose a captain some time.'

'Why?'

As Arabella spoke she accidentally released some ten feet of wet rope, which leapt to attention like an uncoiled spring and thwacked me across both shins.

' "Why?" ' I had anticipated various responses. This was not one of them. I allowed myself an unnaturally long pause, to regroup my thoughts, but also to convey unspoken irritation — I sensed her drift.

'Why what?'

'Why had we better choose a captain?'

The whiff of radical political grapeshot was now unmistakable. We were not discussing leadership qualities but dialectics. The issue was not responsibility for our vessel, but nautical Marxism-Leninism in an unreconstructed canal situation. To win this argument, the intellectual high ground had to be captured.

'Because boats have captains!' I retorted conclusively.

'Because boats have always been run by men!' Fortunately this proved an aside, not the opening of a second front. (All issues of sexism were no-go areas; not only was there an inbuilt majority on one side, but Angus and I liked to feel we belonged to that well-meaning group of male progressives, the feminist fellow-travellers.)

'*Someone* has to be in charge!'

'No they don't. We can discuss decisions jointly.'

'Not if we're going over a weir, we can't!'

I was rather proud of that remark, but it made no more impact on Arabella than did my comprehensive list of continents which, in the absence of captains, would still, I assured her, be lying around undiscovered.

'It'll be chaos. Nothing will ever get done. No-one will know they're meant to be doing it.'

'We can organise rotas. And have meetings to plan each day. It's no problem.'

'Oh sod meetings, Bella!' Trixie staggered by, in mortal combat with a now slightly damp lilo; I smiled gratefully. 'I like a bit of chaos!'

I chose not to follow this up; in the event of a vote, she was obviously the type to spoil her ballot-paper. Instead, I glared at Arabella. 'So the organisational structure of the last two thousand years of maritime history is wrong then?' This was meant as a rhetorical question, and therefore her answer 'Probably' left me little room for manoeuvre.

'They hadn't thought of glass-fibre either, then,' she added for good measure.

'What did you have in mind?' I asked. 'One sub-committee for going to port, one sub-committee for going to starboard?' And, enjoying this thrust, threw in, 'And an AGM for astern?'

'If I'd wanted to spend my holidays on a floating dictatorship, I'd have gone to Haiti!' she said. 'You don't intend us all to salute each other as well, do you?' She tried again, unsuccessfully, to bend the mooring rope to its recommended shape.

'It says on page 2 that we should choose a captain.' That did not sound as authoritative as I meant it to be.

'And does it say where we get the peaked cap?'

Susan came over. 'I'd like to be captain.'

I was surprised by her sudden assertiveness — and her choice. 'See! *She's* not a fascist,' I said to Arabella.

'Then I could order you both to shut up! You've given me a migraine with your squabbling!'

At this point, Angus intervened from the helm, now feeling proficient enough to steer and talk at the same time. (As this was adequate qualification for some people to become US Presidents, he was clearly captain material.) I was relieved; at least his contributions were usually calm and rational.

'I suppose it would be on papyrus, would it?' He got no immediate reply, all of us being as uncertain of the question as of the answer. He turned in my direction. 'These early naval records. On staffing. I remember reading Hakluyt once, on the sixteenth century. Everything down to how many potatoes Raleigh gave his crew for lunch. But as for this dawn of maritime history . . . that'd be original Kontiki documents, would it? Love to read those. British Museum, I suppose?'

Exasperated, I tried not to sound defensive. 'Well, when I said two thousand years ago I wasn't speaking as an archivist! Obviously! I was just referring to a well-known tradition, that's all.'

'Well known by whom?' asked Arabella, who clearly believed that the Rules of Evidence applied to all private conversations. 'Pre-Christian societies were often collectivist, you know.'

'Not on boats, they weren't!' I snapped.

I began to feel my moderate, reasonable 100% normal position was starting to disintegrate in the face of this fanaticism. Suddenly, a flash-back from schooldays came to me. 'Take the Roman slave-galleys!' I cried triumphantly — and, of course, regretted the example immediately. Arabella mimed a whiplash, and curled her lip in a matching gesture.

'I vote we have a slave each!' said Trixie, stirring things happily as she passed by again, trying to remove yet another lilo from the gathering spots of rain. This was not easy, as Arabella's rope lay everywhere, haphazardly, like intestinal evidence of a recent disembowelment. 'I should give up trying to coil it,' she said. 'Just cut it into equal lengths and stack it.'

Angus looked back at the tangle behind him. 'There

must be a page on ''How To Coil A Rope'' in the book.'
He gazed around. 'Probably a whole chapter.' I was about
to announce the page number when suddenly, and with
great force, Arabella and I were thrown several feet astern
and Trixie toppled over onto her latest lilo. The barge
had come to an unscheduled stop. Angus had just demonstrated that he was not yet proficient enough to steer and
talk and look backwards at the same time.

Attention switched from the abstractions of captaincy
and refocussed upon the direct hit which Angus had
scored on the canal bank; we waited for a gurgling sound
(other, that is, than Trixie's laughter), but we soon came
to realise that, give or take a bit of paintwork, both boat
and bank were probably tourist-proof. (Although possibly
the tourists were not boat-proof.) Angus was, admittedly,
unfortunate. The section of canal leading out of the lagoon
has been carved deep into the hillside and is so excep-
tionally narrow that two-way traffic is impossible for a
considerable distance; to enter the canal unscathed here
is like expecting a novice bowler to hit a single stump
with his first ball. Indeed Angus, his attempt to carve
a parallel route North having failed, then used a full
over's worth of run-ups in his efforts to get out of
the lagoon. And so, when at long last we, the only
collectively-run barge operating on the French waterway
system that summer, did eventually enter into the canal
proper, and thus the holiday proper, a small but heartfelt
cheer went up.

This historic moment was also marked by the individual
droplets of rain joining forces and falling as individual
bucketsful. At first, we continued to occupy the regulation
happy holiday positions as per the brochure photos;
indeed, we exhibited a determination to remain upon the
flying bridge which would not have disgraced a British
war movie. But as oilskins were buttoned up and hatches
were battened down, enthusiasm for the sun-deck dropped

with the barometer. On either side of us, the steep man-made slopes rose up like railway embankments, blocking all views except of the sky, which only had on show one giant and very comprehensive black cloud. And so, regretfully, as the Burgundy rain became more and more full-bodied, we slipped below — literally so in the case of the others, who had not read page 7 on suitable shoewear for wet decks.

The engine controls were switched through to the State Room where, with a strong sense of bathos, we turned on the windscreen wipers. And there, cabinned together, we sat hermetically sealed against the storm and the world. Leaning on the formica table, condensation forming on all the windows, we gazed at the cooker and the sink and the washing-up. The boat continued to chug through an unseen land. Little was said, apart from Trixie's demands for a game of cards, and the only clue that we were not in a caravan on Canvey Island was the sight of Angus at the downstairs helm. The permanent throbbing of the engine mysteriously added to a sense of disorientation, and helped explain why such sounds are often the Muzak of interrogation techniques.

Luckily, we were not too cramped, as our numbers were now down to four. At the time of the crash, Susan had been below, taking a tablet for her migraine; the impact had unfortunately thrown her against the medicine cabinet, and caused her to suffer a severe nose-bleed. She had therefore been obliged to retire aft, where she lay abed, gazing at the ceiling and clutching a wet flannel.

Meanwhile, in the group for'ard I sensed a metaphorical migraine. Postponement of the much-recommended pastoral delights; deprivation of the pleasures of grapes turning purple and flesh turning brown; absence of folkloric experiences; all combined to create an atmosphere of anti-climax, of torpor. Also, somewhat irrationally perhaps, I felt a personal responsibility for the arrival of low pressure over Eastern France. Added to which, I knew that, but for me, we would all be out enjoying a Continental Sunday, fraternising, socialising and buying pepper. I tried to assuage the guilt.

'Still,' I said cheerily, 'at least we're in the dry!'

'Lock ahead!' cried Angus.

CHAPTER SIX

It was, in fact, more than a lock; it was a double lock.

For some weeks, the operation of a lock had replaced vampires and bankruptcy courts as the principal cause of waking up sweaty-palmed and panic-stricken in the middle of the night. I had read and re-read the theory but, in my experience of matters physical, no causal link has ever been established between theory and practice — after all, a complete mastery of, say the theory of cycling rarely prevents one's rendezvous with destiny and the first ditch that appears. And it was my view that giant lock-gates and thundering water would prove particularly unamenable to theory. Indeed, ideally, were it not contrary to French canal tradition, I would have resorted to porterage and had the barge carried round the locks by local peasants, in exchange for trinkets from England.

'And a cottage.'

French locks, unlike English locks, have a keeper in residence, a paid warden of the waters. This provoked a further crisis of confidence. The lock-keeper should — according to our rule book — be advised of one's approach by a prolonged blast of the horn. However, the last thing we wished to draw attention to was our approach; welcome though assistance might well be, the great advantage of the English lock system is that one can accidentally sink one's boat in complete privacy. Equally inhibiting was the prospect of his reaction: whatever the small print of his job description, to be dragged from a warm *pot-au-feu* into the howling maw of a now torrentially wet Sunday afternoon in order to service mad and incompetent dogs of Englishpersons did not seem conducive to a happy lock-keeper. One might just as easily insist that a total stranger push one's car for a quarter of an hour.

'A horn does seem rather rude.'

'Yes. Like summoning a servant.'

'Exactly. Wouldn't blame him if he went ape.'

'And made us wait till Monday.'

A consensus soon emerged that use of the horn was alien to the more sensitive Anglo-Saxon culture. Instead, it was agreed, by a lock sub-committee, that Trixie should be sent ahead as our advance warning system and PR rep; the theory was that her self-evident shortage in the arm department and her rare command of CSE Oral French chat-up lines would elicit a warm sympathy. (For Trixie, it seemed, the great attraction of France was that Gallic rhymed with phallic.) An eager Trixie waited in the bows until *Beaujolais Deux*, advancing slowly with a diagonal progress strongly reminiscent of a yacht, next struck a glancing blow to the bank, and then she bravely leapt ashore. Watching her go, I did have doubts. She was an enthusiast of the more *outré* fashions and, in choosing her holiday wardrobe, an outdated concept of what the modern *matelot français* was wearing had led her into an unwise emphasis on stripes; as she turned along the towpath and plodded off into the storm, I felt she was unlikely to evoke the appropriate over-sexed Gallic response as long as she looked like a mobile Belisha beacon.

In fact, to be successful, she would probably have had to look more like an elderly Maurice Chevalier. Because out of the cottage came an ageing spinster.

It was not, however, Mother's Day, but yet further evidence that, in France, ageing spinsters form a Fifth Estate. They are found repeatedly, and disturbingly, in unexpected niches of power. In the hallways of apartment blocks, they operate as a cheap, modern form of draw-bridge, denying access to all but the most favoured. In gentlemen's toilets, they impose standards of hygiene beyond the power of carbolic, and their brooding presence usually stops the average English bladder dead in its tracks. In public places, they normally say little except *M'sieurdame* and possess a silence evocative of the Sphinx. Their numbers and their influence would suggest that the French, so often a maverick world power, are secretly running a genetic engineering programme aimed at creating a master race of Old Ladies.

Fortunately, we could soon tell, even at a distance, that our spinster was not a member of Hell's Grannies, Burgundy *chapitre*. As we clambered about the deck, rustling like crisp-packets in our virgin waterproofs and gathering up fistsful of all available rope, we could detect smiles and bonhomie in two languages coming across open country from the cottage door.

We nosed self-consciously through the lock entrance-gates. Pinpoint accuracy is the key to success in locking procedures, and approaching sideways is not the method favoured by professionals. With a lot of engine noise and froth, Angus — who had repeatedly tried to relinquish his post upon sight of the lock (but had failed to muster the necessary quorum) — determinedly forced the boat along the lock wall. This was, in fact, 90 per cent successful, although there were Jeremiahs amongst us who questioned whether the remaining 10 per cent of the boat should not also be in the lock. During the discussion on this, Arabella, for whom subjugation of the ropes had become a personal mission in life, went astern and hurled a loose collection of them some five feet towards the lockside bollard ten foot distant. As these lay curled on the water like dead conger eels, the propellers were restarted and began to thrash greedily just out of reach. The boat tried to edge backwards out of the lock, and various people began to shout 'You bloody idiot!' at each other, thus indicating the egalitarian staffing structure of the vessel.

'M'sieursdames.'

A sweet, wrinkled face beamed up at us. The English language is no match for the formalities of French protocol, especially under circumstances of stress, and we all sort of nodded and shuffled our feet and vaguely muttered 'Bonjour' and 'Hi!'

'*Vous allez loin?*' she asked, although it was not clear from the tone whether this was politeness or disbelief.

'She says she's surprised to see us,' said Trixie.

'Tell her the English don't mind the rain,' I replied, hoping to convince the others.

The old lady beamed at us again, and then carefully walked the length of the lock, past the juddering barge, to the gate machinery, displaying throughout a tact which suggested that even had we been the first all-nude barge of the eighties, it would not have been something she noticed. What we noticed, however, was that, in closing the massive lock-gates, she manhandled the ancient iron ratchets with a deftness which outclassed any canalwise macho-man − and made our ineffectualness an even greater cause for discomfort.

Discomfort was, in fact, fast becoming the theme word

of the day. It took three of us to frantically drag the mooring-ropes out of the water, leaving our hands alternately white with cold and red with chafing. And then, as we wrestled to loop them around the bollards, they drained their surplus contents down the armholes of our waterproofs. To handicap us further, the deck acted as a skid-pan, the ropes acted as snares, and the bollards acted as lethal stumbling-blocks. And all the while, it continued to rain with a ferocity that promised to fill up the lock faster than it could be emptied. In the general mayhem, although we luckily managed to detect in time Arabella's enthusiasm for reef-knots − which would have suspended the boat rather dramatically, if unorthodoxly, in mid-air as the water-level fell − we failed to identify correctly the bollards around which the ropes should be looped. Consequently, when the water flooded out of the front gate-paddles − immaculately and effortlessly cranked upon by our OAP − the boat, being adjacent, was plunged into a Grade 2 whirlpool, causing it to rebound off each side of the lock like a winning pinball shot. Faced with the choice of going down with the ship and Angus or letting go the ropes, we let go the ropes, though only after a valiant struggle, during which unfortunately Susan was pulled over and dragged full-length through a not very clean puddle. By the time the levels were equalized and the gates opened, the sum total of our achievements clearly suggested to Madame that broken-armed Trixie was merely one of an entire crew who were defective.

As the boat emerged, its sun-beds and holiday bicycles in disarray, I remembered from somewhere a description of locking as 'like trying to park during an earthquake'. The quote seemed inexact, as it omitted any mention of also being in a car-wash at the time. Nonetheless, the boat, despite everything, still appeared to be intact.

'I'm sure that qualifies us for some Clare Francis award,'

I quipped to the others as we climbed back on board.

Answer came there none, because at that moment we saw the next, rather larger, lock. Looming.

And there followed twenty further minutes of the same comprehensive, drenching humiliation — witnessed once again by our lady of the lock, guardian of them both. There was a general conviction that we had reached the low point of the holiday, albeit less than one hour after its start.

Eventually, the nightmare over, we lined up to shake hands and to bid her a heartfelt farewell; our lone Sunday odyssey across the empty rainswept landscape was just beginning. But the old lady paused, something clearly on her mind.

'*Vous allez loin?*' she repeated, with the air of slight perplexity that had stayed close to her features during each of the operations.

I gave her the name of the village with the gastronomic delights, which my researches *touristiques* had uncovered.

She shook her head. '*Mais non, monsieur. C'est pas possible.*'

'*Comment?*'

'*Pas possible. Pas aujourd'hui.*'

Even on those of us with a record of ignominy in O Level French, the words '*pas possible*' had a noticeably downbeat effect. Worse, further interrogation revealed '*pas possible*' to be effectively the password of the day. For slowly, phrase by phrase, in the pouring rain, we translated out of her the information that *aujourd'hui* was an occasion of great import: *aujourd'hui* was the day of the Presidential Elections. And, interrogation revealed, on such rare aforementioned days, universal suffrage and the historic democratic rights of lock-keepers meant that the French canal system closed early.

We had one more question. 'How early?'

She checked her watch. '*Dix minutes, monsieur.*'

This, at four miles per hour, meant that the distance

59

remaining for the day's pleasure-boating was a maximum of 1,300 yards* (barring accidents). It also meant a limited selection of choice mooring-spots for the night. In fact, it meant mooring in the middle of nowhere, in the middle of the afternoon, in the middle of a storm, and without any black pepper.

CHAPTER SEVEN

'Two thousand, five hundred and fifty-six to one,' I repeated, checking once more my ballpoint calculations on Susan's tissues. 'Two thousand, five hundred and fifty-six to one!'

No-one spoke. Trixie re-wiped a small section of condensation from the window, and peered out again into the dark.

'How could *anyone* foresee it, with odds like that?'

Arabella flicked her cigarette ash onto the sizeable remains of her ratatouille. Susan coughed.

'I mean, once every seven years, it's not exactly a common occurrence.'

'You keep telling us how you're the great organiser,' said Arabella, with an uncalled-for sneer on the personal pronoun.

Another lull descended, and the gas-light continued to hiss unchallenged.

A drop of water fell quietly onto the Camembert from an unidentified piece of underwear. The State Room which doubled as a bedroom was now trebling as a Chinese laundry, and every one of the day's garments, except for Trixie's plaster, was to be found hanging somewhere, steaming. Outside, however, the drops of water were anything but quiet, and for five hours the sound of a million drum solos on the roof had not ceased. Taken overall, the scope for dynamic group activity seemed limited.

The face-down P.D. James and the abandoned New Statesman crossword offered clues that individual activities were also on the decline. The highly desirable narrow boat — authentic, historic, aesthetic — represents perfection as a boat . . . except in one respect: its narrowness. Whilst fold-away fitments have become a miracle of modern technology, the state of the art in fold-away people lags well behind, and five living, breathing, smoking, coughing, farting human beings in a confined space can fairly soon impinge upon each other. Indeed, had the State Room been a prison cell, Arabella would have had our case up before the European Court of Human Rights before you could say 'slopping out'. As it was, classic symptoms of unnatural behaviour patterns were already developing: Trixie had challenged all-comers at noughts and crosses (in the condensation on her window) and Susan kept starting sentences with the words 'I-Spy . . .'; neither occurrence is commonly found outside of mental institutions or large families.

But eating away at us was more than simple ennui.

'Here they come again!' cried Trixie.

We saw the lights before we heard the horns. And then, from car after car after car, in jubilant discordancy came the distant but definite sound of the unrestrained French klaxonner. As we watched through the window, a dozen or more smudged beams of light wound erratically along an unseen road and snatches of wild revving reached us across the dark waterlogged fields. The procession had no clear direction, other than some ill-defined lap of honour, and the raucous two-tones lingered on as it hooted its way through hidden hamlets like a triumphal wedding-party.

Triumphal it was, but the celebration was not a private one — it belonged to the majority of France. Literally. Because, for the first time in the history of the Fifth Republic, indeed for the first time since 1936 — according to the static on our Walkman — France had a Socialist President. And all across the nation, it crackled, a giant party was under way, as everywhere left-thinking people cheered and embraced and danced (or at least splashed) in the street . . . except, that is, those in remote canal backwaters.

'Of course, the position of the French left on defence is particularly interesting,' said Angus, whose own protracted silence was principally the result of his early evening study period.

'Oh?' said Trixie, sounding particularly uninterested.

'Yes. It's obviously an historical spin-off of their *la gloire* mentality, but ideologically speaking it's a national aberration.'

'Bloody French!' said Trixie.

'It raises some absorbing questions, the extent to which believers in a supra-national political philosophy are still victims of the historical baggage of their own culture.'

'Mmmm,' someone commented.

Angus paused, while he conceptualised further. Outside, in the night, each of us knew Burgundy to be one vast hospitality suite for anyone who cared to partake; an occasional head twitched wistfully towards Trixie's gap in the condensation.

'Every tribe has its totem pole,' I contributed, mindful that a well-placed platitude is always a useful marker until the conversation comes within intellectual reach again. And, struck by an afterthought, I added, 'De Gaulle was theirs!'

'I think that's right,' said Angus. Before I could explain that what I had in mind was a cheap and offensive remark about the man's shape and nose, he went on, 'He's the root of their maverick foreign policy concepts, their obsession with independence. The heritage of wartime occupation — that's why you have an idiosyncratic socialism here.' Taking a mouthful of cold ratatouille, he warmed to his theme.

Beyond the portholes, our moorings creaked and tautened in the storm. And beyond the moorings, the brambles thrashed wildly as sudden gusts whipped to and fro. And above the brambles, the statutory poplars bent their defences and let the wind have a good howl through their branches.

Angus widened his reference points of historical baggage to include the political storm of 1789. And for good measure added Rousseau. The Walkman spoke of huge crowds in the Champs Elysées.

'I was too young for Coronation Night,' said Trixie. 'And I missed VE night through not being born.'

Arabella got up to percolate some exotic coffee-beans and change the smell in the cabin. The percolator glistened at us. By now, even the most inanimate objects had worked up a fine head of sweat.

With Angus pausing to check a reference, a personal concern as to the microbe level in the cabin atmosphere was expressed by Susan, who had seen the effect of *The African Queen* upon Katharine Hepburn.

'Try not to breathe in and out,' I advised, handing over her tissues.

Somewhere in the far distance, the Klaxon Voluntary was heard again.

'As far as one can tell,' continued Angus, in his overview of post-Louis XV history, 'the philosophical structure that underpins political movements is of unusual importance to the average French citizen.'

'So is a good piss-up, by the sound of it!' said Trixie, increasing her reputation for non-conformist thought. (In fact, gazing around the mist-free sections of the table, it looked as though the British could make as good a case as the French for idiosyncratic socialists, since in one small State Room the political spectrum stretched from Trixie, a militant anarcho-sexualist, to Arabella, the Laura Ashley faction of Marxism, via Susan of the New Statesman crossword tendency.)

'The intellectual content—'

'Look! Fireworks!' cried Trixie urgently, smearing hard at the glass. We all (except Angus) crowded around her, trying eagerly to get a clear view of the far-off light in the sky, showing an excitement that was rather excessive for fully-grown adults. Indeed, it would only have been justified had the light been accompanied by three distinguished old men on camels. But it indicated well our frustration.

'Probably lightning,' said Susan, in a tone which suggested that she had started to worry about the electrical conductivity of canal barges. She sniffed unhealthily. 'Why have all these tissues got biro on?' she asked irritably.

'How far *is* it to the nearest town?' demanded Trixie, betraying a desperate optimism.

'About five miles as the duck flies,' I replied.

'What a pity,' Arabella said pointedly, 'that we're not still with the car.'

I smiled sweetly. 'But think of the environmental damage of using it.'

'What, are you thinking of going into town?' asked Angus, the desirability of this idea not having struck him before. Energised, he went on, 'We could find out what the locals think of the election! What social changes they want Mitterand to make! Oh yes, the cafés'll be packed out by now!' Gripped by enthusiasm for Corbigny's Left

65

Bank, he exclaimed, 'What an historic night to discuss politics with the man in the street!'

This was unfortunately a desire which finally stretched the tolerance of his captive audience a concept too far.

'You don't speak French!' snapped Arabella. 'You wouldn't even recognise *l'homme dans la rue* without a bloody dictionary!'

'That doesn't matter! Human beings can always communicate with each other — by signs, gestures, expressions.'

'Not philosophy and political history, they sodding well can't! So shut up!' she stormed, shouting on behalf of the silent majority.

This was decisive. After a brief polysyllable or two, Angus fell silent and sat back (at least, as far as one could sit back, given the intransigent nature of the seating). He did not raise the socio-political structure of France again that night.

The night, however, was still young. And it was already filled with an unspoken awareness that one would find noticeably better morale in a lifeboat. Also present was an uneasy feeling that conversational storm-cones had been hoisted, and in the consequent caution we all began to address each other with such inoffensiveness that we could have sold the dialogue to the Reader's Digest.

The coffee of exotic origin was mostly drunk in silence. Attention had started to focus on the pervasiveness of the evening's odours. The pungent sauces, the ponging vegetables, the potent onions, the cooking oil, all hung in the air as tangibly as the still-damp clothing; by morning, we would have the world's first ratatouille-flavoured underwear. (The much more pressing pollution issue, viz. my proposal that cigarette-smokers be obliged to travel steerage-class, I felt it tactful to adjourn; Arabella

66

and Trixie, the appellant smokers, had intimated earlier that a democratic forum was inappropriate for the issue, and had proposed instead a bare-knuckled fist-fight over ten rounds.) Eventually a consensus emerged that the night's most rewarding — and probably most action-packed — activity would be to clear away dinner.

As a time-spending, fence-mending group venture, all hands turned to the tap and the washing-up liquid. It took all of five minutes. And then we were back around the table again.

Even back in licence-restricted England, it was still not chucking-out time. Trixie suggested a game of cards, but no two people knew the same game; the old stand-by, Trivial Pursuits, had not yet been invented; and, given the earlier urgent need to remove all wet clothing, the even older stand-by of strip-poker would have suffered from a definite sense of déjà vu. Considerable interest was expressed in noughts and crosses, but one amongst us felt they lacked sufficient educational content. In the end, it was Susan's years at the BBC which provided the answer.

And this is why it was that while, outside, the rest of France riotously celebrated a unique landmark in post-war European politics, and the population fell historically sozzled throughout the land, Angus, Arabella, Trixie, Susan and I sat, brows furrowed under the dripping undies, ears closed against the drumming rain, and wrestled until the early hours with the exacting challenges of Animal, Vegetable and Mineral.

Shouldn't you go swimming outside?

CHAPTER EIGHT

I lay awake in my bunk listening to the sound of Burgundy's average monthly rainfall until the early hours. The only consolation this held was that one day, in some high-class English eaterie, I would be able to confidently reject the '81 Burgundy, and explain confidentially to my guests that the local grape had suffered extensive storm damage that year. In the meantime, I tried to pioneer a technique of counting sheep jumping over locks. But Trixie's distant fireworks came closer and proved to be Susan's lightning, bringing with it loud bangers. Eventually, I abandoned the sheep, put on the bedside light, and counted the locks instead. For the first time, I realised that the return journey, Corbigny/Auxerre, involved the alarming total of 114 locks, or put another way, 8 locks per day for 13 days, or put a still nastier way, 1 lock for every 60 minutes of an 8 hour day of a 7 day week. *And* we were a day behind. And by the time Arabella got up, we would be a day and a half behind. I decided to suppress these figures in the interests of crew morale.

By now physically and mathematically exhausted, I switched off the bedside light again — leaving God in charge of the flashing outside light — and finally, soothed by the rhythmic drumming of hailstones, managed to fall into the arms of a distant relative of Morpheus.

When released next morning, soon after daylight, it was to the depressing sound of still more rain. But the first indication that something was seriously wrong only came when I wiped the porthole and realised I could not see land — in any direction.

My immediate reaction was that our 17 granny knots, 12 reef-knots, 8 bowlines and 47 half-hitches had inadvertently come loose and somehow we had entered the Fastnet Race. Fortunately a more in-depth wiping revealed that the towpath and the canal were still with us, but that the whereabouts of the surrounding lower countryside would require a major police search. I gazed around. Overnight, sward had become swamp. Yesterday's fields were today's floods and the only life visible was isolated cows standing on isolated mounds, looking mournfully as though they were having to strain their cud before chewing it (with their cheese to be presumably remarketed under the label *La Vache Qui Nage*). The grey, swirling expanses of murky water bore a remarkable resemblance to the apocalyptic visions of grey, swirling expanses of murky water that had led me to reject a life on the ocean wave in favour of a nice, safe canal holiday.

Trying to resist an urge to panic, I leapt sharpishly from my bed. But upon landing in an inch of cold water, I decided not to resist the urge any longer.

'Christ!' I shrieked. 'We're sinking!'

This was so effective in getting Susan out of bed (despite her overnight onset of flu) that I knew at once I had discovered the ideal way to achieve an early start in the mornings.

'Aah! It's freezing!' she cried as her feet hit the water.

'Sorry. Did you want to wait till it's warmed up?' I grabbed just my dressing-gown, conscious of the people who have died in floods and fires whilst trying to pack their life's belongings into a set of matching valises. 'Come on! We don't want to go down with the boat!'

'Isn't that what captains are supposed to do?' she asked, splashing her way behind me to the cabin door.

'They're supposed to show leadership!' I retorted, leading the way into the corridor.

At this point, a soaking wet and naked Angus put his head around the adjacent door. 'It's the shower,' he said apologetically. 'I think I've blocked the drain.'

Ten minutes later we were all oilskinned and on the bridge, surveying the dramatic watery scene. We had persuaded most of the errant shower-water back down the plug-hole; the problem of submerged rural France was more intractable. As we leant at 45 degrees into the wind and watched the nearby river Yonne put in its bid to become the world's seventh ocean, one sensed the sun-deck might be surplus to requirements for a while longer.

'So May is the ideal month, then?' purred Arabella, maliciously echoing my sales-pitch in England.

As we stood watching what appeared to be climatic history in the making ('Bring On The Icebergs!' demanded Trixie), the only conceivable explanation seemed to lie with President de Gaulle. For I now recalled, as a student back in cobble-strewn '68, hearing him rally the nation against revolution and socialism with the stirring declamation, *'Après moi, le déluge!'* At the time, I had innocently put this down to the classical traditions of French rhetoric, but the simultaneous arrival, thirteen years later, of a Socialist President and the inundation of France did seem to be stretching coincidence a little far. Given de Gaulle's semi-divine status, it appeared eminently reasonable that he should have been put in charge of world weather upon his death and ascension. I explained this theory to the others.

'You're saying our only hope for fine weather is a recount?' asked Susan, whose ill-health appeared to have done little damage to her tongue.

There seemed little purpose in staying at our mooring, proud though we were of the knots. Indeed, there seemed little purpose in anything, but I had a daily quota of locks to fill (and empty), Arabella felt us unlikely to receive a personal delivery of hot *croissants au beurre*, *and* we were all up. And so *Beaujolais Deux* moved on.

Confining though the boat was, no-one appeared keen to explore beyond her. Although the exquisite old villages of rural Burgundy seemed to have been designed with 20th century tourism in mind, that morning we gave them all a heavy rain-check. As we chugged past the various small settlements I would call out, 'Anyone for the château of Théodore de Bèze?' . . . 'Anyone for the birthplace of Jules Rénard?' and be received by philistine silence and a shake of sou'westers. Arabella showed interest in the village of Marigny, but only because it boasted a baker and what the multilingual guidemap called a groger, and Trixie, now at the helm, regularly enquired, 'Are you *sure* you can't go by canal to Majorca?'

If granted the desire to be elsewhere, our differing tastes would have boxed the compass. Susan would have demanded a sandy beach in the detective section of an open-air library (where even the disintegration of the ozone layer would not come between her and the dénouement of a Ruth Rendell); Angus would have rerun his previous year's trip: a cycling tour of the industrial heartland of Belgium (not yet available as a package holiday); Trixie would have chosen a twenty-four hour duty-free shop staffed by Latin toy-boys with sun-tan beyond their boxer-shorts; and Arabella would have voted for a Cuban co-operative, preferably specialising in the manufacture of avant-garde jewellery. The present attractions of the French canal system, on a scale of one to ten, would not have registered.

In fact, all the lower-deck talk was not of day-dreams but of such matters as fender-positioning and the finer points of bollard usage. After the previous day's locking fiasco — people have shot rapids with greater dexterity — we all felt the need to be nautically redeemed. For mile after mile, we clustered around the handbook's illustrations of a lock — drawn to a scale which suggested their forthcoming issue as postage stamps — and tried to seek enlightenment as to the true nature of gate-paddles and reverse thrusts. The desirability of a slow approach, the rotatability of propellers, the inadvisability of falling in, the pros and cons of tipping, all went into a think-tank melting-pot on The Lock. And indeed we had mastered a technique which was just about word-perfect . . . when the voice at the wheel announced the presence of a bridge. A manually-operated bridge.

*　　*　　*

The inhabitants of the little village of Dirol still speak of the day when five strangers chugged into town and tried to raise their drawbridge; they speak of it as the most remarkable chaos caused by a bridge since the Allied Forces failed to take Arnhem.

The trouble began when, being unable to discover the word '*pont*' in any of our reference works, four of us went ahead of the boat to investigate. Speaking with the benefit of hindsight, we should have tied up the boat first. As it was, we reached the iron bridge, off which iced rain was pinging like grapeshot, barely fifty yards in front of *Beaujolais Deux*. And since the boat was now single-handedly in the single hand of a most hapless Trixie, it continued to advance as unstoppably as an ICBM beyond the point of recall. Energetically, we examined *le pont mobile*.

The mechanics of pre-war manually-operated bridges are not unduly complicated, but we were a crew raised more in an artistic tradition — meaning that, whilst I could pen a short essay describing a bridge, and Trixie could restore a Canaletto painting depicting a bridge, and indeed Angus could elaborate on the existential aspects pertaining to a bridge, there was none of us could actually make one work. In fact, this type of basic drawbridge is simply held in place on one side by weights; these are released by hand, and then pulled up by chain — thus raising the bridge. Working as a team, the four of us cracked the theory of the weights, triumphantly released them . . . and then watched our side of the bridge spring up to just above our eight outstretched arms. It was at this point that we realised the significance of the chain — which was on the opposite bank. Which could not now be reached on account of the bridge being half-up. Or, from the advancing boat's point of view, half-down.

A wrinkled old man, who had silently observed the entire proceedings from the open upstairs window of an equally wrinkled old farmhouse set on the aforementioned opposite bank, allowed himself a knowing smile, shook his head sadly, and then, leaning on the window sill, settled down to await events. All of us made graphic gestures to him, indeed performed several charades worthy of award, in trying to elicit assistance for our desperate plight; he made no attempt to stir — although he did nod to Trixie as she passed by. One sensed a soul permeated for generations by the reading of Maupassant and holding to the firm belief that rural tragedies were the centrepiece of provincial life and should be allowed to unroll without interference.

Into the frame came *Beaujolais Deux*, and with her came our plaster-casted Trixie still at the helm, looking like a panic-stricken Lord Nelson and using her free arm to semaphore the rough equivalent of 'England expects the effing boat to sink'. As we ran up and down the bank shouting 'Backwards!' the gap began to close with awful inevitability and, like Number Two, we began to feel our salvation lie in the safe haven of insurance. In response, Trixie continued to cling to the wheel and thrust regularly at the throttle control with her groin, but she achieved little apparent effect, except possibly for sexual satisfaction, and the only pertinent advice remaining seemed to be 'Jump!' But then, at the very last moment, in a valiant effort to avoid slicing off the admittedly redundant sun-deck, she executed what skiers would immediately recognize as a stem Christiana, and succeeded in slewing the barge sideways and providing a useful new amenity for the locals in the form of a pontoon bridge. This was short-lived, however, and before we could take advantage of it, she had revved the boat violently through a further ninety degrees, stalled it in mid-stream — to a second knowing smile from the upstairs window — and started to drift slowly back towards Corbigny and, more appealingly, home, leaving us stranded on the bank, her stranded on the boat, the boat stranded in the water, and the bridge stranded in the air. Only the rain was unaffected.

After a few moments, two more aged inhabitants, supplied, from the look of them, by Central Peasant Casting, emerged from nowhere, to stand and stare and shake with laughter. It was, however, good-natured laughter — responding, no doubt, to a performance that had the simple appeal of an old Buster Keaton movie — and, once they had got their breath back, they offered a helping hand. And with several long, strong pulls on the chain they made the waterway a fit place for boats again. We expressed our grateful thanks, but what they expressed, in impenetrable dialect through gaps in much penetrated teeth, will forever remain a mystery.

The task of retrieving our boat took a little longer; Trixie's ability to come on command to the bank would have won her few rosettes had she been competing in a dog show. Back aboard, despite a widespread enthusiasm for recriminations, it was agreed that no-one was to blame for the latest fiasco (a verdict always favoured when it is felt that everyone is to blame), since there had been no committee responsible for *ponts mobiles*. There was, though, a strong movement in favour of mutiny, thwarted only by the procedural difficulty of having no captain. By now, however, all ambitions for that post were evaporating, replaced by a new keenness to be Mr Christian, whose good fortune in spending his voyage ashore was much envied. With the sun-beds starting to mulch down and the fun-bikes continuing to rust, it was decided to follow his example and go ashore for lunch at the next village.

CHAPTER NINE

Making land is the great excitement of an ocean voyage. But making a village is, in *non-socialiste* weather, the recurring pleasure of a canal voyage. No settlement has settled in the same way and, at little more than a hundred yards a minute, the unknown that lies around each bend has time to fully massage the imagination. At Chitry-les-Mines an elevated château dominated the scene, at Marigny life clustered around a church on a knoll, at Dirol there was but Main Street, straggling like a Wild West frontier townlet. Of Monceau le Comte there was no sign at all, apart from a sign.

Three bollards and a small canal lay-by gave an oblique hint of its existence, a guide-map symbol of half-a-plate and knife and fork gave the only clue to its attractions. Monceau le Comte itself lay several hundred yards east, wedged between the Yonne, at this point swollen but unburst, and the small valley road running parallel. The outskirts of little Monceau were inauspicious. In olden times settlements deterred visitors by building a high wall and ramparts; nowadays they achieve the same effect by surrounding the place with chalet bungalows. But leaving the through road and plunging inwards revealed the fifteenth and sixteenth centuries to be alive and well and living in decaying splendour. The ancient houses still clung to an erratic medieval layout, and various of the cobbled lanes were accessible only on two feet or 2CVs, a car whose suspension mysteriously predates the existence of roads. In the village's tiny central square, which was neither central nor square, stood a barely-advertised *auberge*, entered by an outside flight of stone steps.

We made a joint beeline for the fading *tabac* sign. We knew, before leaving England, that, as gastronomy on the grand scale was ruled out by having pockets on the petit scale, the hopes and aspirations of our stomachs lay with the traditional family restaurant. And if, as gourmet Arabella asserted, the quality of their cooking is in inverse ratio to the modesty of their façade, then here we could reasonably expect even the left-overs to be worthy of Ronay rosettes.

We crossed the façade, and immediately our stomachs sank at the sight of the bare bar, with its statutory *marc* drinker and a decor rooted in post-war austerity; *la specialité de la maison* was apparently not the hungry tourist. But before we could act on second thoughts we were shown a second room and found ourselves in not so much a family restaurant as a family dining-room, homely and welcoming, where time had also stood still despite the presence of an impressive grandfather-clock. The feel was somewhat reminiscent of those almost-vanished pubs of rural England, where the bar is the parlour, and the signal for closing-time is the appearance of the landlord in pyjamas.

'M'sieursdames.'

A smiling grandmotherly figure of great age (the retired lock-keeper breed) emerged from the hall, and fussed us solicitously to a table in the empty room. A simple, handwritten menu, almost free from multiple-choice questions, was placed before us. All the great French chefs genuflect to the regions, and each of the regions buries its treasures, like truffles, deep off the *routes nationales*; we all sensed instinctively that, with my nose for local flavour, we had discovered a rare restaurant and chef who, were they in England, would provide endless source material for the Good Food Guide's ever-vigilant contributors.

'*Ancienne* rather than *nouvelle cuisine*, I suspect,' whispered Arabella, a trifle superfluously.

Already, I could foresee the prospect of her compiling a detailed list of every ingredient, which would then be followed by the loss of another twelve hours spent shopping.

But the arrival of the *potage du jour*, whilst undeniably hot and steaming, raised trickier questions than simply '*ancienne* or *nouvelle*'. For, somewhat unexpectedly, it proved to be alphabet soup. At first, not being entirely *au fait* with local specialities, we nurtured a hope that this was traditional Burgundy fare, a viewpoint strengthened by the apparent discovery of a circumflex amongst the vermicelli. On closer digestion, however, it turned out to be merely the top half of a letter Y. Knowing this, every sip we took was a cultural disappointment.

Unsure whether we had hit a bad day, or whether the philistine tastes of the English stomach had preceded us to the kitchen, we called over *la patronne* when we had finished eating up all our letters. Arabella to the fore, we explained our desire to partake of local delicacies and emphasised the sophisticated nature of our palates. She smiled delightedly, and named a *plat du jour* quint-essentially (I translate loosely) Burgundian which she promised to prepare for us.

She was to be as good as her word, but what the word

meant, we were quite unable to establish. Asked to describe the dish, it did not clarify matters much when she re-enacted what appeared to be a ritual disembowelment (though it did loosen one or two of our own stomach muscles). So we refilled our glasses, savouring the local vintage we had insisted upon, and awaited our speciality. Unfortunately, not only was the food's name without English equivalent, but the arrival of the food itself provided no clue either. In retrospect, it was the moment when the old lady, age slowing her movements, carefully placed our plates in front of us that we first began to suspect our epicurean zeal might have over-reached itself. By contrast with the English, the French gourmet is a free-thinker, operating on the farthermost frontiers of food (as a nation, they eat anything that moves − and, in some cases, while it is still moving) and using the world's most advanced digestive tract. Consequently, in front of us we found a delicacy which, by its dubious shape and disturbing odour, strongly suggested an object whose consumption in England could constitute an arrestable offence; it would certainly cause any relevant Elizabeth David recipes to be sold under plain brown paper.

As she returned to the kitchen and we prodded at what, days later, we would come to know as pig's intestines or − presumably in non-family restaurants − chitterlings, a feeling in our own guts told us that the most desirable method of disposal was not going to be internal − as a veteran of sheep's balls in North Africa, I was particularly well-placed to recognise overwhelming odds. We did, however, have our public reputations as *bons viveurs* to consider. (The shameless desire of Susan to demand Heinz spaghetti-rings as an alternative was overruled.) Angus argued that, since the human body was merely an intermediate stop in life's great recycling plan, we should just streamline the process and discreetly drop lunch *en bloc* down the café bog. (This also was overruled as, given the strictures of the French toilet system against such insolubles as Tampax, we feared the addition of a plumbing surcharge to our bill.) For a while, we tried Arabella's suggestion that we cut the food up and re-arrange it around the plate in a new context; it was, however, a short-lived suggestion as each slice of the knife also gave our noses a strong clue as to what the pig itself had last eaten as a *plat du jour*. And so in the end, to achieve dinner with honour, we were forced to commandeer Susan's tissues, and to wrap and zip the lot in a shoulder-bag, for removal as a throw-away take-away.

Madame re-entered. '*Vous avez bien mangé?*'

'*C'était excellent, madame. Compliments au chef.*'

She beamed. The reputation of the English abroad rose.

It was a hungry, cold and wet walk back to the boat (Angus called it the retreat from Monceau) and our dejection was becoming pathological. No-one said much, although Trixie hiccuped a lot. I also noticed, as I thought through the afternoon's itinerary, that she and Arabella had developed a rolling gait. This was not so much a naval affectation as two carafes of local *vin extraordinaire* on an empty *estomac*, and, before the canal chart had even been rustled, they were slumped onto the State Room seats with all the body language of fixtures and fittings. Reluctantly, I prepared once more to play the role of the irresistible force, but seeing my lips about to move, Trixie announced a desire to lie on her sailor's bunk and listen to the rhythmic, timeless swishing to and fro of alcohol in a glass.

'Hear, hear!' said Arabella. 'I think everyone should have a siesta.'

'All day!' added Trixie.

'Every day!' added Arabella.

'Without ever getting up again till the sun comes out!'

'Hear, hear!' said Arabella.

81

As self-appointed lock counter, I was aware that so far our tally was only nine, our evening target twenty-four: a lot more water had still to flow under the day's bridges. I set about being geeer-up-in-chief, enunciating the forthcoming villages of Cuzy, Chevroches, Coulanges, Prégilbert, as if reciting a list of explorer's aphrodisiacs. They responded as if listening to a list of explorer's diseases.

'I expect the sun's out in Auxerre,' I said.

'Liar!' said everybody else.

In the end, civilized persuasion having failed, I invoked the disputes procedure and a vote was taken. The on-goers beat the stay-putters by three to two; the vanquished agreed to show a grudging leg at the locks; and the wet ropes were cast off once more. As I eased *Beaujolais Deux* out into mid-waterway, I offered up a silent prayer ('for all those in peril on the canals') and begged the patron saint of barges for an entire afternoon free of incident.

There would appear to be no patron saint of barges. The next incident occurred after approximately eight hundred yards.

Here, rounding a tree-lined bend, we came across our first fellow-bargees, a well-spoken, middle-aged couple from Surrey, moored by the towpath, whose marriage had been destroyed by their holiday.

In a partisan version of events supplied exclusively by the wife, now separated (the husband currently living in their Volvo Estate, parked some four feet away on the towpath), we learnt that their boat had not moved for the last ten days — making our own rate of progress seem positively reckless. Indeed, their boat had not moved since lunchtime on Day One, when the husband, courtesy of a rope coiled Arabella-style, had unexpectedly tripped and fallen into the canal — an event causing him to remember that he could not swim. The canal only being

82

a couple of feet deep, this would not ostensibly seem a handicap, but apparently his discovery that canals were composed of water had so unnerved him that he unilaterally (if metaphorically) dropped anchor and announced the holiday to be terminated forthwith. His wife, the sole crew-member, had objected to this, but did not, unfortunately, possess the same bargaining rights as those evolved in our own barge's constitution. The dispute had then escalated. She had refused to abandon ship until such time as the rental expired, and he had stormed off to collect the family Volvo from base camp. Upon his return, vigorously waving maps of the Home Counties, irrevocable words had been exchanged, intransigent positions taken up. And there they remained, throughout the days of never-ending downpour. It now only required the boat to be cited as co-respondent and the tragi-comedy would be complete. (The tragic elements of this matrimonial impasse did not, however, weigh too heavily upon Trixie, whose cry of 'Any chance of a lift home in the Volvo?' was, I felt, lacking in tact.)

For a while, I jiggled in and out of neutral, trying to keep the boat stationary in the hope of obtaining a statement from the other party, but he remained in the car, ostentatiously hidden behind the pages of a *Daily Telegraph* and leaning well back in the fully-reclined passenger seat.

'I allow him to use the toilet,' said the wife, not wishing to seem in any way unreasonable.

For some reason, this provoked a stream of unTelegraph-like abuse, and she broke off the conversation to return a collection of insults of her own. '—ing drown' and a '—ing holiday' appeared to be recurring topics in the interchange. This was judged an appropriate moment to move on, and we departed unnoticed.

As we turned into the next bend we could still see them, each occupying their entrenched position, and still hear them, each peppering the towpath with volleys of marital invective. Coming, as it did, at the virtual start of our journey, this strange encounter took on a curiously powerful symbolism, vaguely reminiscent of blind soothsayers prophesying doom at the beginning of Greek tragedies.

We hurried on into the storm.

a Shadow!!

CHAPTER TEN

The night was spent near Cuzy. It was yet another early heave-to, brought on by sheer weather fatigue — and a mooring site opposite a bar. (This decisively swung the balance of power against the on-goers.) During the social activities of the late afternoon and evening Angus again failed to establish the epistemological approaches of French intellectuals but he did learn about the alcohol capacity of Burgundian peasants in a bar. Consequently, by breakfast time there was the considerable problem, in the words of the traditional canal-shanty, of 'what shall we do with *three* drunken sailors, earl—y in the morning?'

I went for a walk, alone. I had now made it my habit to check the quality of each new delivery of rain — if it bounced below the knee the forecast was categorised as hopeful. Also, I was curious to see Tannay, a small hill-town two unbending kilometres away and up; described by the guide-map's innocent translators as a 'gay wine city', it promised a nearby château and a 14th century church. And, in addition, I needed time to plan a re-allocation coup of the barge's accommodation. Susan and I had opted for the aft cabin in a tactical move to avoid smoke and smell and sex in public; it was now clear to me the strategically correct move was to occupy the for'ard cabin, and gain permanent mastery of the boat's controls . . .even if that did mean cancer, cooking-oil poisoning and twice-daily performance of popular erotic acts.

Tannay was an attractive town, in a more than attractive position. I checked out the church, walked round the square, looked round the shops. In deference to the time, I indulged myself in a hot chocolate and some very crumbly croissants. And then I looped my way back around the recommended chateau at Pignol. When my excursion had, I reckoned, allowed time for even the dead to get up and have a decent wash, I made my way back down towards the canal.

As I came within sight of the boat, I noticed that my body cast a faint but discernible shadow on the wet road. With impeccable timing, the sun began to make its first watery amends; and as it did, all my half-drowned ambitions for our holiday schedule began to come excitingly back into focus. With less than impeccable timing, I noticed the other four make their exit from the boat.

'Thought we'd visit Tannay,' called Trixie, in a remarkably misplaced show of initiative. 'Coming?'

I stood my ground. 'No. Nothing there worth seeing. I wouldn't bother.'

Unfortunately, Arabella had already seen the guide-map's supermarket trolley symbol stamped on the town, and no amount of disparagement poured on 14th century architecture was effective. And the arrival of fresh dry air gave the group outing a new zest. Although my presence might have speeded the ransacking process, the uphill road to Tannay had an unmitigated straightness that would not have disgraced a runway, and my feet could not face the journey a second time. I went back to the boat, alone.

And waited. There are few places on the Canal du Nivernais which could be described as ugly, even fewer as an eyesore. Unfortunately, most of these places are situated one hundred yards up the Tannay road. At this point, a level crossing, a railway crossing, a railway station, what appeared to be a marshalling yard, and what was definitely a huge corrugated multi-storey warehouse covered in either cocaine or concrete dust, combined to reduce the visual amenities of the area. For a while, in the first flush of sun, my preoccupation was less how to align my lilo than how to strain it. But by the second hour on the sun-deck, the aesthetics of the location were undermining any uplifting thoughts. By the third hour, I was mentally drafting a critical appendix on Tannay environs for the *Guide Bleu*. I was also sorely tempted to issue a 'lost persons' notice to the gendarmerie.

The deck temperature was well into the seventies, and mine was approaching boiling point, when the wanderers finally returned; appropriately for the hour, they were laden with lunch. Nonetheless, by now even the sight of eight varieties of gherkin was far from an effective peace-offering. But somehow the unique weather produced a unique unanimity: the prospect of eating an alfresco buffet while cruising gently through the meadows had an appeal for everyone (except Angus, whose housing Ph.D. led him to view open countryside as a failure of urbanisation). This buffet prospect also had an enticing visual imagery: us as participants in a sort of updated '*Sur La Grande Jatte*'. But whereas Seurat had placed his famous holidaymakers upon the river bank, we would be elegantly profiled against the passing countryside. I could envisage us, as we sat on the raised deck and worked our picturesque way through the salad, forming not just a *tableau vivant*, but a *tableau mouvant*, indeed a rare *tableau mangeant*. Or, as Trixie, our classical art expert put it, 'We can chug and chew at the same time.'

As Susan and I secured the tablecloth to the deck with vintage cheeses, Angus unknotted the mooring ropes, and Arabella prepared to inaugurate the flying bridge position. The boat started to froth away from the bank. In the distance, as if on cue to be rustic, we made our first sighting of a fisherman, immobile on his stool. Beyond the cool shadow cast by the stone arch of the road bridge, the full bright brochure-like light of rural Burgundy shimmered ahead of us. *Beaujolais Deux* edged her thirty-nine blue and white feet into centre stage of the canal, we raised our glasses to the sun, and Arabella thrust the engine controls up to full throttle. And nothing happened.

*   *   *

To be a grown man, sitting, helplessly, beside a broken-down vehicle, for hour after hour, in full public view, utterly dependent upon the arrival of the cavalry from some distant garage, is, I always feel, an experience that ranks second only to sexual inadequacy in the hierarchy of failure. But to be *two* grown men, indeed to be two grown men and three professedly practical grown women, sitting in the aforementioned situation, confers such a range of group humiliations that it would cause any Japanese crew to fall stomach-first upon a ceremonial boat-sword. Worse, from the very moment when the engine first shuddered into its terminal silence, we all knew instinctively that it was a crisis quite beyond the powers of five people who could not successfully raise a drawbridge. And rumour also had it that, although a Renault 4 may be bump-started, the same remedy, even in only two feet of water, is hardly applicable to six-berth barges. There had been no choice but to unwrap our asterisked note of Mayday phone numbers.

Nonetheless access to a phone was still a considerable problem — indeed, for over half an hour the operator could have been more easily contacted by Verey pistol since *Beaujolais Deux* had, like the day before, unerringly chosen mid-canal to go floatabout. In fact, we had so little steerage-way we could have been out-manoeuvred by driftwood; had the fisherman been more alert, he could probably have claimed salvage.

Good advice was in short supply on board. Trixie kept saying, 'My kingdom for a sea-horse!' and then giggling helplessly; Arabella claimed to have seen a film in which a table-cloth was brought into dramatic service as a sail; and Susan simply rubbed in more sun-tan oil, turned a page, and said how peaceful it was without the engine. It took endless patience, excessive swearing, all of Angus's limited prowess with a boathook, and a personal demonstration of why I had been my school's under-12 long jump record holder, before we reached land again — where I vigorously hammered in two iron mooring spikes to prevent any further escape by the boat.

Fortunately the French have the answer to phone-box vandals — the phones are usually placed in cafés, where they can only be destroyed by the much rarer, more ambitious, café vandal; we were therefore able to make our *coup de fil* from the canalside bar. Unfortunately, the phone-call itself was not an unqualified success. The good news was that we got through; the bad news was that we got through to Number Two.

'Stopped? . . . . How do you mean? . . . "it stopped"?'

Never, as an eleven stone weakling, do I feel that sand has been more effectively kicked in my face than after an encounter with a mechanic. But the discussion of a breakdown by telephone precludes even the tattered dignity of being able to point at offending, unnameable parts. And Number Two certainly lacked the practised unshockability of an AA switchboard.

'What do you mean? . . . ''and then nothing happened''?' He paused, to allow large exclamation marks to travel down the phone. 'It couldn't just stop!' (He punctuated even the shortest sentence with unmistakable sounds of chewing, so that no-one be in any doubt a pleasurable lunch was suffering disturbance.) 'You must have done something!' I mumbled innocence. He responded with a heavy-duty grunt that helped mould his silence into an intimidatory scepticism. I waited, guilt mounting.

The sound of air being pointedly expelled came through the earpiece. 'Where are you?' I gave him directions. He made little comment, though I heard a female voice off.

'How long?' I dared to ask.

'Couldn't say,' he replied, with the air of a man about to do justice to a siesta.

Altogether cast somewhat low, we left the shade of the café and went back once more to the great floating outdoors. Our lilos and loungers still encircled the tablecloth and the cheeses still held it down. But stationary, as an immoveable feast, and with a light industrial backcloth, the lunch had lost its charm. By now, many of the lettuce leaves were short on crunch and, with the warmth of summer another degree closer, the wine had become *chambré* enough to suit a low oven. As afternoon encroached, we fitfully nibbled and niggled the time away as best we could. Discussion of the possible contents of the warehouse was to the fore, sparked off by debate as to whether 'excrescential' was a figment of linguistic imagination or kosher OED. Trixie and Susan disported themselves, but dispiritedly. Occasionally a lorry would rattle across the level crossing, occasionally a hornet would investigate the pickled gherkins, but little else of excitement, or interest, happened. Time passed by. Trains passed through. Fish passed on. We passed caring.

I took a stroll the few hundred empty yards to Cuzy. The road was now dry, although in a nearby field the swings and slides of a playground still stood culottes-deep in stranded floodwater. In the little village it was siesta time and no-one stirred — possibly they snored, but the old stone walls were too thick to tell. Tucked by the T-junction, two gendarmes sat sleepily in their blue paddy-wagon, waiting with wild optimism for traffic violators. For a while, I too loitered, out of a bizarre suspicion that I might witness the world-renowned *flic* tradition of insensate brutality being visited upon some unsuspecting klutz with a defective indicator. But nothing, not even a speeding ox-cart, disturbed the peace.

I loitered my way back to the Canal of Despond. There, spirits were sinking below the Plimsoll Line. After four hours of hot tetchy *ennui*, even Pooh-stick races were losing their appeal (canals being noticeably short on current, some two dozen sticks were still jostling neck and neck at their point of entry) and all of the sun-worshippers, no matter how uninhibited, had come up against the finite amount of body available for tanning.

'We could build a raft,' said Trixie. I detected whimsy.

'Perhaps we could apply for eight gramophone records,' suggested Susan, who preferred security.

'Which ones?' asked Angus, spotting an opening for a rare application of intellect.

'My luxury object's a dildo!' said Trixie, closing the opening.

At that moment, the classic lines of a 2CV van, the only vehicle ever manufactured with built-in baguettes, lurched onto the towpath at speed, tipping at an angle which would have given Isaac Newton second thoughts about his views on gravity, and advanced towards the boat with its famous whining impersonation of an under-powered hairdryer. It drew up alongside us and the hairy legs of Number Two rippled muscularly onto the soft-packed earth.

'Always thought this one was more of a suicide mission than a holiday!' he called up, in what clearly passed for his idea of jocularity — his was not the non-judgmental approach of the caring professions. Wimpishly, we smiled back.

Boat-lovers, like Exclusive Brethren and horse-lovers, have time only for that section of humanity similarly besotted; dedicated to a life afloat, and obsessive enough to regard God's creation of the land as a planning error, in their world landlubbers figure only as some form of unfortunate wrong-turn in the evolutionary process. It is also an incestuous world, full of private buzz-words and esoteric nautical know-how; we lacked the Arran sweaters and the lean to windward and the smell of salt-spray on our underarms, and we knew it.

He flicked aboard a bulky bag of tools and made his way enginewards; several of us followed, trying to recapitulate the dying moments of *Beaujolais Deux* in as disingenuously self-exonerating a manner as possible. But Number Two was not one for small talk — or indeed for big talk — and his only reaction, when faced with our defunct engine, was to give the well-known, long drawn-out 'mechanic's sigh', a form of breathing which cogently expresses utter disbelief at the folly of the world. That done, he then prepared, with a nicely-perfected little touch of weariness, his daily wonders to perform.

Discretion being the better part of embarrassment, we returned to our stations. But, with our pride needing almost as much salvage work as the boat, his presence provoked in us an unexpected burst of artificial activity, and everyone began to do seapersonlike things, and to be shipshape, and to generally look as though a sea-shanty might be imminent. Indeed, for the next hour or so, whilst macho-man massaged the heart-beat of the boats engine, he did so against a background of figures urgently scrubbing the decks as if entered for the Captain Bligh gold medal award, of yet others pumping the bilges clean with a scrupulousness normally only applied to a baby's bum, and of Trixie gazing concernedly over the side to apparently check for barnacle growth. In a fit of *folie de grandeur*, I even tried to come to an understanding with the ropes — which were, as yet, still undomesticated. It is hard to see why so much praise is heaped on the Indian rope trick; the real miracle is not to get the damn things to stand up, but to make them lie down.

Early evening was coming on, and the cicadas were having a last leg-rub before bed, when Number Two emerged from the hold. He wiped a butch smear of engine grease from his cheek.

'All done,' he announced.

We thanked him, and he made his way across the refurbished, and all but re-keeled, *Beaujolais Deux*.

'Try not to let it happen again,' he said, somewhat unnecessarily.

We nodded. Arabella asked him what the cause of the trouble had been.

'Excessive speed,' he replied.

I searched in vain for a trace of irony around the mouth. He flicked his tools back into the van, and vibrated away without a backward glance.

As we stood on the no-longer burning deck and watched the golden sun sink behind the warehouse, I calculated that we were now 19 locks behind schedule.

There's half a baguette in the carburettor

SNAFU

CHAPTER ELEVEN

Prospects, however, at last were looking good. The evening balminess was of the quality that ensures satisfied barometer-tapping; the current scenic situation was a definite incentive to movement; and Arabella was keen to discover new shops. The only potential hiccup, or, to be more precise, the only potential belch, lay in the majority wish to partake of the hair of the dog that had savaged them the night before.

In fact, everyone wanted a drink, and not just to forget the emotional trauma of our breakdown. Angus wanted to try and forget he had no serious discussion since England; Trixie wanted to forget she had no serious sex since England; and Susan wanted to celebrate she had not been ill for 24 hours (a state of affairs she was able to remedy between two and four a.m. that very night). Arabella, on the other hand, seemed to feel her enthusiasm for alcohol was political: only by increasing her wine consumption could she directly improve the lot of the downtrodden peasant viniculturist; on this issue her commitment was total. For myself, I merely drank to relieve the strain of unrecognised command and the worry that no-one would get up in the morning, because they were drunk.

It was for once — and once only — a false fear, although that owed less to our restraint than to the café-owner's desire for an early night. We had been good customers — good enough to have given him a strong business motive to sabotage the boat — and we had even proved it was possible for the English abroad to enter a bar without immediately setting about its destruction to the tune of 'Awa' the lads!' And indeed, the hospitality had no more been issued in half-measures than had the drink. Nonetheless, some of our party did present rather a high-voltage culture-shock. Trixie's idea of evening wear betrayed a feel for colour co-ordination that suggested an international maritime distress signal, which warned, it would seem, of imminent personality disorder. As the evening wore on, Angus's desire to discuss publicly the meaning of the universe and related issues (in fractured French) merely came across to regulars as the one true indicator of the irredeemable drunk. And quieter (indeed silent) but no less disturbing, Susan developed a shade of white for which doctors and publicans recommend a five-yard exclusion zone.

It was, therefore, still a civilized hour when the shutters came down and, with slurred bonhomie all round, we stepped out into the moonlight. Contrary to the odds, no-one fell over, no-one increased the work-load of the local cleansing department, and no-one tripped into the canal. It was a lovely starlit night — though fully appreciated only by those few of us still able to simul-taneously look upwards and walk forwards — and for once, encouraged somehow by the tranquillity, it was early to bed.

It was also early to rise, for the total absence of heavy

drumming rain made it difficult to sleep. In its place, warm, dazzling chinks of sunlight flickered across our faces. And so, without alarm calls or personal abuse, by 08.30 hours we had all washed and partially dressed and completed a light fuss-free breakfast.

And then we all went up on deck, with the strong desire, one sensed, that this time we should get things right, that we should depart in the way Nelson and Number Two would have wished. And, in a memorable first, we did. Trixie gently coaxed the engine into life, I deftly unhalf-hitched the aft ropes from the aft mooring spike on the bank, Angus firmly pushed the stern out with the boat-hook, I equally deftly unhalf-hitched the for'ard ropes from the for'ard mooring spike, Trixie manoeuvred the boat into the middle with precision, Arabella coiled the ropes into an area of less than three cubic metres, and *Beaujolais Deux* got smoothly under way in what even Pythagoras would have considered to be a straight line. With a few basic techniques at last beginning to gell, we made good, steady progress through the morning, through the fixed bridges, the loose bridges, the single locks, the double locks, the bends, the kinks, and then, having reached an idyllic brochuresque village, complete with grizzled *boules*-players in action on a small, tree-lined square, we decided to tie up for an approximate elevenses. It was the moment when I leapt ashore with the mooring ropes that it struck me we were supposed to have brought the mooring spikes with us . . . and not left them embedded in the bank by the road to Tannay.

Several anxious minutes passed while it seemed the boat might be doomed to wander the French canal system for the rest of time − or at least for the rest of the tank − but fortunately the village of Villiers also boasted bollards, and to these we became extremely attached.

'Well!' said Arabella, and paused. My culpability was so self-evident that she realised all comment was superfluous . . . but after further consideration she decided it was an opportunity too good to forego.

'Well!' she said again, 'I know some people have felt progress has been a touch slow, but how exactly does going backwards help us?'

I ignored this thrust. 'Anyone for *boules*?' I asked airily, hoping the witty historical allusion* would generate a similar sang-froid.

'*Boules* yourself!' said Trixie, less wittily.

'Perhaps a brioche or two,' said Arabella sweetly, stating the price of silence, and the five of us trooped off to the bread shop.

It was the village's only shop, and run — as all Burgundy seemed to be — by an elderly lady. The premises were short on supplies but long on hospitality; unmodernised, cavernous and cool, a long wooden bench and table stood on the flagstones in its empty quarter. We ordered coffee and convened a committee.

Its rapid upshot was that I found myself volunteered, nem.con. except me, to undertake emergency spike retrieval duty. It was not exactly a prestige appointment, especially since, as the trip meant *l'auto-stopping*, my selection was also the result of being declared the candidate least likely to suffer sexual harassment from French motorists. (Even so, I was to be nearly taken into lay-bys more than once by drivers who, having had explained to them the nature of my mission, felt it unwise to laugh and drive at the same time.) Uniquely, despite my role as a holiday time-and-motion expert, my enthusiasm for instant action was muted.

* * *

Standing, waiting, with head bowed and thumb erect, by

* Drake

the side of a dusty foreign road, on the edge of open country, was an experience not indulged in for over fifteen years. It should have meant nostalgia, bringing happy memories of free lunches, 500-mile lifts, memorable personalities, and an address book full of exotic place-names. However, I was no longer a hairy back-packer, with 'student' stamped on my poverty, and with my appearance promising a high-grade cultural exchange to all-stoppers. Instead, I was an unshaven man of early middle age, of foreign origin and with no worldly goods on display — and therefore self-evidently a fugitive either from Interpol or paid employment. Despite this, I made reasonable speed on the outward leg — indeed, to see fields and woodlands flash past at more than four m.p.h. was quite heady. The real difficulty came on the return journey, when I discovered that Continental drivers have a psychological block about giving a lift to such a man carrying two iron mooring spikes.

To be precise, I made about the same progress as the Waffen SS would have done had they tried to hitch-hike their way into France in 1940. Except this time the resistance was slightly stronger since Cuzy's two gendarmes, their conviction rate wilting in the heat, looked upon the sight of an alien in apparent possession of two jemmies as their best chance of promotion since the riots of 1968. Their ritual incantation having drawn a blank, my explanation of these objects as being 'for making holes in banks' was, in retrospect, an unfortunate choice of words. Consequently, it took all my Anglo-Saxon charm and some gifted barge impersonations before it was accepted I was not a crime wave and allowed to continue my journey. 'Continue' was another unfortunate choice of words, for a long hot hour passed, followed by another, during which I had as much luck trapping vehicles as did the police. And in the end, I became the only member of the crew of *Beaujolais Deux* to have the unexpected bonus of a walking holiday of Burgundy.

But the solitude was not without its compensations. Four days into the holiday, and the only common denominator so far found among the crew was British passports, and the only common interest, arguing. Angus's rural Scottish origins had, it was becoming plain, left him not only with an unfortunate allergy to all countryside but also a Puritanism that made him increasingly fractious about the limited holiday interest in self-improvement. This put him repeatedly at odds with Arabella, whose high-mindedness now only surfaced when sober, an increasingly rare condition, and whose waking hours (an almost equally rare condition) were spent in pursuit of a standard of living last seen at the court of Louis XV. By contrast, Susan, of whom I had held high communing hopes, never willingly left her lilo, and was suffering from some condition for which she had to take four detective novels a day; any interruptions, any ill-timed locks, any requests for movement, invariably brought her out in rash statements. As for myself, the continuing collapse of my best-laid plans had produced a tetchiness normally associated with vitamin C shortage on slave-ships. And in the midst of all this, Trixie was still, bizarrely, pining to be a couple! Indeed, being a free — and frustrated — agent, as well as owner of a multiple-edged tongue, she was increasingly exercising her barbed *bon mots* with the abandon of a scatter-gun. I was beginning to feel that ABTA should, under their charter, be obliged to provide free personality testing for all group holiday bookings.

Villiers still looked idyllic and peaceful and timeless when I limped through with my spikes in the late afternoon. In the flower-filled smallholdings only the shadows and the occasional goat had moved; in the little orchards that stretched down to the canalside the autumn supply of cider had perhaps inched imperceptibly closer; in the cobbled yards the ducks quacked more sparingly than ever. It was the archetypally sleepy French village, where one can hardly tell the difference between weekday and Sunday, between siesta and non-siesta, between life and death.

The cry of '*Achtung! Achtung!*' was therefore somewhat unexpected, especially when heard while crossing the deserted village square.

The forerunner of various unpalatable consonants to ricochet across the water and into the sleeping village, it was, in fact, the evidence that *Beaujolais Deux* at last had company. Indeed, apart from the unfortunate vessel whose crew had been immobilised by hydrophobia, the sight of a newly-moored and privately-owned *Kanalboot* constituted the very first proof that holiday life could exist on the canal. And predictably enough, it was Europe's number one travellers, the real hard-core tourists: the Germans. For them, there is no track too unbeaten, no desert too unsignposted, no bowel of the earth too deep (and no canal too wet), but that they are there, making it a land fit for travellers' cheques, and pioneering the way not for the homeland but the home movie. The presence of such hardy companions was a comfort, a reassurance.

They were at a neighbouring bollard, and I strolled up, waving my spikes, to exchange canalfarers' news in the time-honoured fashion; handy tips and boathold hints are the *baguette* and *beurre* of a life afloat.

'Hallo!' I called out.

'Nix good!' they called back, several generations of the family pointing Auxerrewards, and shaking their heads in Teutonic unison.

And then, before I could seek clarification, their family limousine drew up. I was still working on my greetings when they offered me their farewells, and I found myself watching as, with gestures of despair at the French heavens, they steadily transferred all their sausage bags, two sausage dogs, a large acreage of lilos, the latest

101

holiday hi-fi system and several kilos of unused sun-tan lotion from the boat to the boot. It was a quasi-military operation, and they were a family I would have been proud to have served under. Nonetheless, as I – now joined by all except Susan, who was engrossed in a fictional dénouement – stood and watched them pack, it was with great sadness that we gradually realised we were witnesses to probably the first-ever post-war German tourist defeat. And that soon we would once again inherit the water.

'Nix good!' they repeated enigmatically, and waved goodbye.

And then, with traditional, and admirable, German efficiency, the family positioned their car and their boat at respective ends of a small concrete slipway, joined the one to the other with a tow-rope, engaged forward gear, released the handbrake . . . and slowly, but steadily, the car moved away and backwards down the slope and into the canal.

* * *

Although we had already lost over half the day un-necessarily, the prospect of watching a well-heeled but surprisingly highly-strung German family try to remove a barge and half an Audi from a canal in the middle of nowhere was considered uniquely irresistible. We cracked open several local wines and made ourselves comfortable up on deck. And for the next two hours every available in-habitant made the effort to visit the scene personally and express a carefully-weighed opinion. For some, this was merely '*Zut, alors!*'; for others, it was the rubbing of a grizzled chin and an elaborate mime of some recondite engineering technique. But no-one missed out. Indeed, all the village's *boules*-players re-arranged their evening schedules to be on hand to give advice. Even the elderly lady from the village shop took the trouble to cross the bridge and slap her thighs. We could have sold tickets.

Eventually a local landowner, exercising an immaculate thoroughbred on his nearby meadows, trotted up and a deal involving a tractor and a sum seemingly not unadjacent to the Marshall Plan was painstakingly negotiated. After a lengthy pause, probably to allow the notes to be counted, a large tractor — of the sort supplied free by the Common Agricultural Policy to all European food-producers, including gardeners — trundled throatily into view. A complex and detailed discussion on load-bearing factors and the quality of German bumpers (*Vorsprung durch Technik* was a quip much favoured by the gathering crowd) then ensued — as calculations progressed, an alarming rumour that congealed sun-tan oil had the specific gravity of concrete gained ground — and a quantity of heavy-duty chain sufficient to subdue even Houdini was doled out.

And then, with the local population lining the bridge, a series of chains were attached, and a series of bets were placed. Asked to express a personal preference, the majority would, I suspect, have opted to see the tractor join the car and the barge in the water, but, after much blue smoke (and, it seemed, similarly-coloured language), the dramatic little daisy-chain of vehicles slowly clawed its way up on to dry land. An extended ripple of applause greeted their appearance from the vasty shallows. Some of these shallows, however, came up with them, and, to comprehensive German *épatement* and widespread French *schadenfreude*, a steady cascade of greenish slime paid glowing testimony to the cubic capacity of the car interior.

The cleaning-up process, though, had less drawing power as a public spectacle, and once the scenes of emotional trauma and German wallet-beating had run their course, village life began to make its way back behind the shutters.

A lovely sunset beckoned, and we decided to take full advantage of our mooring spikes and find a lovely rural setting to match. I took the helm, and, as we moved through the lengthening shadows, a pair of kingfishers zig-zagged their way ahead of us in high-speed fluorescent courtship; a little further along the overgrown towpath, and there, equally dazzling but in absolute immobility, stood an ancient *pêcheuse*, all in deepest white, and protected from the last rays of the sun by the wide brim of a straw-hat that began life in a Renoir painting. A small wicker-basket and a fishing net rested beside her; I slowed to a speed appropriate to anglers and nineteenth century visions, and a shy smile flickered back in our direction.

A few hundred yards more, and the trees and the reeds and the meadows joined forces to shape the perfect mooring spot. Gently, we edged in to the bank, for once scorning the civilization of a mooring by the towpath, and, glowing a slightly radioactive pink in the twilight, I and Susan, the last on deck, made the boat secure. Meanwhile, the first sounds of the river night-shift began to be heard; by the time we were ready to go below, half the cast of *The Wind in The Willows* had joined in the chorus, and the warm night air was filled with a primeval but powerfully romantic aura.

'He's brought a holiday project with him, you know,' said Susan.

'A what?' A frog croaked nearby, equally startled.

'A group holiday project. Books, articles, for us to discuss.'

'He hasn't!'

'He has! Got it all ready while you were gone.' Below us, a gas lamp hissed into action, and cast an off-white light onto the water.

'Oh no! What on?'
'Unilateral nuclear disarmament.'

* * *

Veritas may well be *in vino*, but as a useful consequence of alcohol it comes a poor second to oblivion. That night, wine was the only deterrent to Angus's armoury of *a prioris*. ('One of our hocks is worth ten of your *post propter hocs*' was how Arabella put it, in a particularly wounding lawyer's exchange.) We drank not to forget but to avoid having to learn; indeed Trixie declared her brain to be temporarily a hardened silo where no intellectual first strike could penetrate. And try as Angus did to construct thesis and antithesis, the rest of us were only swayed by the 12 per cent proof of the *vin du pays*. ('Now the ground rules—' he would begin. 'Don't you mean the ground-to-air rules?' someone would finish, hopefully to force him off his trajectory.) By midnight, I was eager for glad confident and sober morning, and so, having made my slurred excuses, I tottered off and slid onto my bunk.

CHAPTER TWELVE

As usual of late, my dreams took place in a watery world, full of shipwrecks and waves and pirate mechanics, and sleep was a hectic, all-consuming activity. The light of day only came to my attention when somehow I slid off my bunk and then found myself moving with unexpected speed towards the door. At first, having had a troubled night in which the world had seldom ceased to spin, it did not immediately strike me as surprising that the journey from bunk to corridor was downhill. But then (and I recommend this as a cure for feeling hungover) I realised that the earth had apparently shifted on its axis. Straightaway, and in a fairly rigorous spirit of inquiry, I went above (or where *had* been above when I last went below). But the nature of structural changes to the physical world is not always easy to determine, and apart from observing an uncalled-for repositioning of the horizon, I was for some time without an obvious lead. It was only upon discovery that the deck was no longer in the recommended text-book position, i.e. parallel to the water, that I realised we were aground.

The cause was quickly apparent. Overnight rains had tautened over-tight ropes. Which had been tied by persons who wished to remain anonymous.

We were still in much the same place, give or take a yard or two of mud-bank, but it was clear we had either to dislodge the boat or re-align the surface of the canal. A small crew started to gather, several of them under the impression that the local brew had permanently altered their centre of gravity. Initially, it was thought the boat could be refloated by all of us leaning over one side of the vessel, a position we were keen to adopt since a consequence of the previous evening was a general desire to be sick. However, the need to also rock the boat to and fro proved a particularly unmarketable concept, with the result that we totally failed to budge old *Beaujolais* – though an internal litre or two of new Beaujolais did come up. (The command 'heave' was widely mis-interpreted during this manoeuvre.) Next came the boathook. Nearly all of us (Susan had unfortunately slipped a disc in childhood) took it in turns to take the strain, to wedge the thing in the bank and apply untold G forces of accumulated fat to set us free. But all the pelvic thrusting was in vain, and produced scarcely a hint, and certainly not a ripple, of any movement – though there was always the possibility of an unofficial world pole-vaulting record. In the end, all we achieved was a suspected hernia and proof that boathooks float. This just left the Emergency Think Tank. And ten minutes of emergency thinking produced only one idea – that we look up Frogmen in the Yellow Pages.

'Shall I go and get some eggs from a farm? And some fresh milk?' This was not Arabella's idea of lateral thinking, but merely a further example of a derailed one-track mind.

107

'Tell you're a townie!' Trixie said. 'Where did that idea come from, a Janet and John book?'

'What's that supposed to mean?'

'If you want to get milk from a farm these days, you have to flag down a tanker lorry,' I said. (The sub-text of our irritation was that shopping did not seem an act of solidarity at this time.)

'And farmers get their eggs like the rest of us — by queuing up in Tesco's!' added Trixie for good measure.

But it was never a tradition of Arabella's to allow facts to get in the way of her opinions, and we were unable to deter her from setting off on a wild hen chase. Armed with a milk jug and the opinion that one refloats better on a full stomach, she leapt to *terra firma* — which responded by displaying rather more freedom of movement than the boat. For a moment she hesitated since, even to those with 20/20 vision, there was not so much as a tied peasant-sty to be seen anywhere. But, taking a cowpat as her evidence-in-chief that milk-makers were at hand, she strode myopically off towards the farm-free horizon.

The able-bodied thus being down to two, and the mentally-alert to zero, it seemed only a matter of time before the authorities had another *Marie Rose* on their hands; certainly, with the four of us now standing at an angle familiar to the bandsmen on the *Titanic*, but failing to produce their up-tempo tunes, it looked as if there could well be another difficult day ahead. So far no-one had dared contemplate the spectre of Macho-Man, even on the grounds that it takes a hulk to raise one, but he was at the back of all our minds; indeed, he was possibly at the front of Trixie's, since failure to make contact with a male under pensionable age for the last five days appeared to be causing her a hormone imbalance.

My own hormone imbalance was being caused by my latest addition of our lock total: seventeen. A day's worth — and a third of the holiday gone. Our enforced becalming was upsetting enough, but even more aggravating was the knowledge that just a handful of locks distant lay Clamecy. At medieval Clamecy, the only town *en route*, the locks appeared to become thinner on the ground (metaphorically speaking) and offered a rare chance to put one's foot down (metaphorically speaking) and make up for lost water. With a fair wind and a dredger, Auxerre was still not quite a lost cause.

Urged on by this thought, and with the rising mist gradually advertising our shame to a wider world than ducks, I decided to take the plunge (not at all metaphorically speaking), and to try and put my shoulder to the keel.

'Is it a bird? Is it a plane? No, it's a wimp in a Y-front!' cried Trixie as I tested the water.

The romantic aura of the previous night's natural history tape had dissipated with daylight, and as I prodded the sludge only its more primeval elements came to mind. Although I was ostensibly testing the temperature, I would have keenly welcomed research funds into giant leeches, the malarial mosquito, water snakes, bilharzia, electric eels, gas-driven eels and man-eating water-voles; although only the depth of a child's paddling pool, the murk held the contents of my entire subconscious.

'We're with you!' called out Susan, speaking spiritually and having in mind the kind of practical help supplied by a 'Good Luck' telegram.

My feet stirred up puffs of smoky-black water as I stubbed about for a firm footing (through my plimsolls I could feel hard ridge-like objects which suggested to me the skeletal features of an earlier tourist-crew) and gingerly parted the razor-edged reeds as if re-enacting the Moses story; Nature, I felt, occasionally needs help with its public relations. At the same time, the others went ashore to synchronise our muscle-power and to further slacken off the ropes. None of us, unfortunately, had remembered to check the instruction manual at the 'boat aground' page, illustrations section; had we done so, we might have noticed that never, in all the helpful diagrams on refloating, are any of the eager little matchstick figures ever seen *in* the canal, along with the boat. Mine was apparently a unique stance only recommended to barge-hirers should their vessel unexpectedly come under machine-gun fire.

I prepared myself for action, and pressed my quivering body against the hull of *Beaujolais Deux*. Angus strained himself with the boathook, which I had helpfully retrieved, and the other two made encouraging floating noises. And gradually, *Beaujolais Deux* started to ease out of the ooze. I pressed harder. Then, with a sudden squelch, she was free. And, with a sudden ouch, I was lying full-length in the position she had vacated. As I struggled to regain sound and vision, and put the mud back where it belonged, I was aware of footsteps above me on the flying bridge.

'How would you like your eggs done?' enquired Arabella, smiling triumphantly, and carrying a dairyful of goodies.

* * *

We breakfasted on the move. At last *all* systems were go. The weather looked perfect, the engine sounded perfect, and we had all the bits of the boat with us. To add to our pleasure, the already exquisite small-scale scenery had now started to supply steep wooded hillsides, which rose in newly-green splendour above us. There was, though, just the one pervasive fly in the ointment.

The correct frame of mind for a canal is a pottering frame of mind. Just as the watched pot never boils, so a watched lock never fills, nor indeed empties. But all my hourly bulletins on Burgundy's charms-to-come, the prospect that a day or two away lay gorges, cliff-top villages, the finest of vineyards and a possible discotheque, had at last managed to fuel a collective frustration at our painful progress. The Canal du Nivernais, however, is the oldest of French canals — the first sods being dug as the first aristocratic heads started to roll — and so it is operated throughout by an extraordinary variety of pre-industrial machinery, which would appear to have influenced few major engineers other than Heath Robinson; it is not a system designed for speed, or impatience, or anything less than Zen Boatmanism. And soon, with time's winged chariot showing us a clean pair of wheels, and our itinerary close to tatters, we had merely to *see* a creaking, leaking pair of gate-paddles to be given proof positive that a lock raises the pressure of blood far faster than that of water.

Also, the arrival of true blue holiday weather had germinated in each of us (I think) a new enthusiasm for all the nautical miles that awaited exploration. And so when, eventually that morning, with under a quarter of the journey done, and nearly half of the holiday gone, *Beaujolais Deux* and her little band entered upon the last, long tree-lined curve into ancient Clamecy, it was an encouraging landmark, a sight viewed with joy unconfined.

It was also joy short-lived.

At first, we thought it was the sound of distant thunder. Then, as we neared the town jetty, we thought it was the sound of a scenic waterfall. And finally, as we gained a full frontal view of Clamecy, we realised that the stretch of 'lock-free canal' I had detected on our chart was, in fact, a stretch of open river — except that (and here the EEC phrase 'Nix good' started to repeat unpleasantly on my brain) it was currently a stretch of closed river — with possible allowance for

111

white-water rafters. The days of storms, the days of floods, the nights of passionate rain, all were at present holding a reunion in Clamecy. And boats were not invited. The Yonne was surging over the weir and under the bridge and through the town with a force that would have generated enough electricity to keep Paris fully lit for a year; driftwood considerably larger than our *Beaujolais* was travelling at a speed that had eluded Donald Campbell throughout his entire life; the riverside walks were reserved for frogmen until further notice; and the roar of the water was loud enough to activate a suggestible bladder at a distance of over two miles. A few carefully-composed photos, and our friends would think we had been up the Orinoco.

CHAPTER THIRTEEN

We tied up at the end of a small traffic jam. Ahead of us was the entire Saturday contingent from the black lagoon. On the quayside, lips pursing knowledgeably into expressions of gravity, lingered a collection of the town's river experts and their dogs. Beyond the line of boats, and separating canal from river, a very solid lock with very solid gates barred all progress. Astride the metal walkway over the gates stood the latest old lady of the locks, who, with broom in hand and hand on hips, had perfectly captured the posture of a civic Cerberus. And thus it was, as we gazed hither and Yonne, that we at last came to understand the puzzling absence of any boats going South – and also grasped the definite difficulty of anything, bar iron-bound barrels, going successfully North.

A consensus of futility emerged and, back down in the State Room, a proposal for an emergency committee meeting was rushed through all stages. Its agenda called for the interchange of useful ideas. Not surprisingly, there was a lot of silence. Angus's comment, that according to some philosophical concepts of reality it was arguable whether the floodwater could indeed be proved to exist, was followed by a suggestion that he went and jumped in it. Arabella was primarily concerned with the libertarian aspects of the flood, and wanted to inquire into the legal basis for restricting our access to the river — and was equally abruptly thrown out of court. Susan complained about the river's noise and started on another detective novel. For once, Trixie's standard proposal, that we each buy several bottles of pastis, was thought to be the most practical suggestion on offer. We all prepared to go into and around town.

Clamecy was an appealing small town that had clambered up the hillside for centuries. Its medieval core was still virtually unspoilt, to the extent that every second building seemed to be shored up, to prevent its innards cascading down the steep alleys to the market square below. The old quarter brought with it calm as well as charm, for its town-planners, in an enlightened move several centuries earlier, had introduced pedestrianisation by means of long flights of chunky stone steps. (And if ancient architecture was not carrot enough for the climb, an added attraction was that the close-packed buildings came with shade and the view came with breeze — oblivious to irony, a scorching summer sun was now trying to brown off the flood victims.)

But appealing though the town was, it was still small, with a limited number of circuits to be completed, and a finite number of views to be viewed . . . We wandered in and out of the shops. Arrival in any town after days in the outback always has the attraction of a refresher course in civilization, but this too wears off . . . We bought homegrown newspapers. There is always the outside world to be caught up on, and given the speed of international affairs an almost daily check has to be run for new wars that could be personally disruptive — indeed, even in our brief absence the Pope had been shot. (Being in a Catholic country on a Catholic river, it seemed momentarily possible that the excessive activity of the heavens might be some Church-organised retaliation.) . . . We bought and sucked ice-creams. But all this languorous delaying of reality did not lower the river one French iota. So we found a café a few hundred yards from the tumult of the water, and placed a bulk order for pastis.

At first we sipped in silence, listening disconsolately to the sound of bleeping video-games being thumped by French adolescents who also had time to kill. But gradually, as the Devil found mischief for idle deck-hands, our plight, our sense of thwarted destination, niggled its way to the surface.

'Now we know why May is Cheap Rate,' observed Arabella acidly.

'Certainly the month for cheap remarks,' I responded. 'Anyway, even Columbus got becalmed once or twice, I expect.'

'Except he didn't have to take the boat back after a fortnight!' Pleased with this, she warmed to the theme. 'I mean, the King of Portugal didn't stomp up and down the cliffs, shouting, "Come in, No. 15, your time is up"!'

Susan laughed, rather to my irritation.

'Shouldn't that be the King of Spain?' queried Angus, unwisely.

'Oh, don't be such a bloody pedant, Angus!'

'I was just—'

'—being boring!' snapped Arabella. And added, equally unwisely, 'As usual.'

'Fight, fight!' interrupted a grinning Trixie, although whether from a desire to alleviate the tension or exacerbate it was unclear.

'Oh, do stop being childish!' Angus's tone strongly indicated that for her to do so would break the habit of a lifetime. This in itself was dangerous talk, but he then overreached himself. 'Both of you!'

Arabella and Trixie exchanged glances, but it was Arabella, exercising some implicit right of precedence, who replied: she delivered herself of a long, mocking 'oooh!' and then, looking smilingly around the table to associate us all with her opinions, said, 'There speaks the expert on old age. Had a bypass operation to miss out on youth.'

'Oh, that's socially progressive wit, is it?' he countered. 'Most très amusant!' Angus recognised that he had just received the 20th century version of a slap across the face with a glove in front of witnesses but, being by nature short on rapiers, he was obliged to reach for a blunderbuss. 'And what sort of an operation did *you* have, to miss out on intelligence for adults? A lobotomy?'

'Don't patronise me! I'm not impressed by the number of library tickets you have!' An esoteric insult, most would have said, but it was quickly clear that, even had she commented unfavourably on the size of his penis, she could not have scored more points.

'I'm sure you're not!' Angus retorted. 'After all, actual knowledge could seriously damage your thought processes. I mean, a little more reading and a little less fashionable bigotry and you'd have no opinions left at all! Even adolescent ones!'

'Oooh, we are so proud of our grey matter!' She spoke as if to a child. 'But then grey's your favourite colour, isn't it, dear? Grey personality, grey opinions, grey lifestyle! Great grey bloody bore!'

We had gone from trivia to trauma in 9.4 seconds. It was the classic hallmark of the well-established relationship: as all roads lead to Rome, so all rows lead to the

116

same long-running bones of contention. Also, as in all domestic minefields, the object of the game is not to avoid the mines but to explode them in your partner's face.

'At least I get my opinions from thinking!' It was the slur on his brain that had really hurt. 'Not like your pre-packaged radical chic shit! I'm sick of listening to you, you and your matching opinions, all carefully colour-coded, bought in a set. By catalogue, probably. Habitat viewpoints for the "right on"!' The bookworm had turned.

At this point, Trixie, realising the danger of these exchanges developing into a purely private argument, decided to open up the proceedings to all-comers.

'Oh, shut up, Angus! Don't be so bloody pompous!'

'Pompous?' he said, pompously.

'Yes. Like a walking, talking tree of knowledge. Enlightening the plebs. Haven't you sussed the difference between real life and a philosophy seminar yet?' 'Yet' was the visibly wounding word, for it cast a sudden critical light over a decade of unsuspecting friendship. 'If you so much as hear a fart, you want to do a structural analysis of it!'

Arabella giggled. For a moment, Trixie paused uncertainly — Angus was clearly waiting for his blood to return to his brain. She then started to say, 'Even at university' but she was interrupted, and Angus was not about to give way.

' "Real life"? Since when have *you* had anything to do with real life?' I clouded my pastis with water, and gazed intently into it — Angus had just upped the ante by several decibels. He glared at her. 'Your whole life's one long fantasy — if it's not inane jokes, it's getting legless, and if it's not getting legless, it's stupid schoolgirl crushes, and if it's not. . . I mean, you even dress like something out of Disneyland, for God's sake! So spare me your worldly wisdom and act your age!'

117

This would all have been below the belt were it not for the outrageously low position in which Trixie usually slung her belts. However, this technicality did not prevent it being her turn to blanch. She stubbed out her cigarette, resisting the temptation to use the back of his hand, and took a deep paragraph-sized breath.

'We . . . are . . . on . . . holiday,' she said in slow-motion baby-talk; had paper been to hand, Trixie would probably also have drawn a large picture of a holiday to ensure her message penetrated to the maximum possible number of his senses. 'We enjoy ourselves on holiday. We do not train to be professors on holiday. We do not investigate the meaning of life on holiday. We buy tubes of sun-tan oil instead. We unwind. We laugh and smile and relax and have fun. So fuck off!'

'Thank you, Trixie,' said Arabella. 'Well put.' To Angus, she said, 'So, any more "frontiers of knowledge" you want pushed back, any more stupid "concepts" you want thrashed out, may I suggest you go on an Open University camping holiday? Alone. And not clutter up our boat? You bloody windbag!'

There was a brief silence; Angus found himself without concepts of any kind. Noting the powerful two-pronged assault, and its clear 2-to-1 majority, I nodded sagely in the women's support. But, to lighten the atmosphere, I quipped, 'We could have a swear box for profundities!'

It was a mistaken quip. As one dock closed, another dock opened.

'Oh not *more* rules?' said Arabella, slightly in jest, but mostly in sarcasm.

'Think of them as *your* rules,' I said. And, unable to resist, added, 'You like that sort.'

She pretended not to hear. 'I'm surprised you haven't issued us with a rule-book. Hundreds of pages of do's and don'ts. With penalty points.'

I gave her a sweet smile of almost total malice. 'Yes,

I suppose I do prefer to be efficient — but then I just don't have your natural flair for chaos.'

'The rigid authoritarian mind rarely does.' Needling, like fencing, has strict protocol, but now, after a tiring week of bloodless practice, almost every phrase was chosen for its conversational properties of sweaty gelignite. 'Your approach does make for an unusual holiday, though. Every morning I wake up expecting to be given deadlines; and productivity targets for locks; and knot training; and be timed in the toilet.'

'I've never noticed you wake up in the morning. Which morning was that?'

But freelance-mouth Trixie was ahead of her.

'Why *should* we get up in the morning? Why should we *have* to get up at all?'

'Why bother to go away on holiday in the first place then?' I retorted.

'With you? Why indeed?'

She and I were close to A Moment Of Truth, and my answer, 'I thought because you'd been dumped by everybody else!' seemed to move us a little closer to it. Fortunately we were interrupted by Arabella who had a comprehensive supply of her own abuse which she did not wish to see wasted.

'Just because you ordered the brochure for this holiday does not mean you're in charge of the bloody canal!'

It was a hot day. I was starting to feel pastissed. I snapped back, 'And having to learn to tie a half-hitch is hardly an infringement of your constitutional barge rights, for Chrissake! I ask you to moor the boat, and you're worried it creates a legal precedent! Aren't there any laws against being bloody-minded, Miss Bloody Lawyer!'

'You could sell your idea of holidays to the Home Office,' she said. 'They're always looking for short, sharp shocks. Two weeks in a boat with you, and half of England's delinquents would be going straight!'

It was a good thrust. I blustered. ' "Straight" isn't a direction your muddle-headed nonsense ever got the *boat* to go in, though is it? If we'd had someone in *charge*, perhaps we wouldn't have won this year's "Laughing-Stock of the Canal" award. Who knows, you might even have left a lock or two undamaged.'

'You are speaking,' enquired Trixie, 'of the leadership qualities that lost the mooring spikes, are you? That tied us up so we ran aground? That booked the holiday in the monsoon season?'

'Exactly!' said Arabella with relish. '*Male* leadership qualities.' I tried to catch Angus's male eye, but, on account of his wounds, he was now a non-combatant.

'Five days and nights of "We must keep moving! We must keep moving!" — and look where you've got us!' Trixie gestured flamboyantly at the fruit machines. 'Stuck here! *Very* — what was it? — efficient!'

'If I'd wanted to join the Marines,' snarled Arabella, 'I'd have had a sex-change operation. As it is, from now on I want a *restful* holiday. Like Trixie. An unstructured holiday. An unorganised, non-hierarchical holiday. Understand? No more early morning alarm calls. No more time limits on the lilo. No more coiling ropes by numbers. No touring villages with a stopwatch. And no bloody reading aloud of the Michelin Guide!'

'Hear, hear!' said Susan. Most unexpectedly.

Tearing a strip off the Pope's attempted assassination to mark the end of her chapter, she put down her Dorothy L. Sayers.

Addressing me, she said, 'I too have had quite enough of being bossed about. Especially as I wanted to go to Scotland. I am quite capable of steering the boat without your advice. I do not need to have locks explained to me. I know perfectly well what to do with fenders which is more than can be said about you and dirty wash-basins.

And I am also able to do all necessary sight-seeing without leaving my lilo.' Addressing the others, she said, 'Furthermore, I propose we improve the quality of life on board by banning all smoking as from now. I also suggest we reduce the excessive proportion of the kitty that is being spent on alcohol — and spices. And I think that if we all go to bed early in future, everyone will benefit from the extra sleep.' And then she went back to her book.

We departed the cafe a chastened group. When we had entered, we were two couples and a single. When we left, we were five singles — of the ill-matched type that dramatists trap in lifts. And over a week of fun-filled vacation still remained.

We made a silent circuit of the square, as if hoping the sun would also lay the metaphorical dust we had stirred up. Then we cashed some travellers' cheques, and we bought another cornet each, and chose some postcards, and tried to recreate normality. But our original, intractable holiday crisis had yet to be solved, as the constant off-stage roar made only too plain. We visited the lady of the lock and asked her to read the runes of the river. She sighed and spread her hands wide and forecast a delay of two days for those going North. But to go South looked an equal non-starter — immediately beyond Corbigny there rose a ladder of sixteen locks, an assault-course quite contrary to the spirit of the new laid-backness. Faced with this dilemma, we ummed and aahed and agreed decisively to defer decisiveness.

The only consensus available was to return to the boat, which was due a little light servicing. As indeed were we. We ran the engine to recharge *Beaujolais'* batteries, and took de luxe showers ashore to recharge our own. We filled her insides up with pastis-free water, and we inspected her public and private parts, as per the manual. And then, in the shade of the towpath trees, we all lay on deck and waited for the soothing balm of evening to arrive.

Tell you what – let's go
down to the local caff
for a good old bicker

CHAPTER FOURTEEN

Our state of mind was not greatly assisted by being part
of a long line of people awaiting balm. To judge from
the fragments of speech drifting across the water, it was
almost exclusively an assemblage of the English —
clearly, being far from home, the chance to join such
a familiar institution as a queue had been irresistibly
comforting — and, to judge from the fractured language
ricocheting across the water, almost all their boats were
fitted with children. Unfortunately, of all social group-
ings, the family unit on holiday is the most unstable so
far developed by the human race (with a half-life of only
a few days, it is a rare family group that survives a full
holiday intact) and the behaviour patterns of these particular children strongly suggested they would not be
allowed back into England under the current rabies
legislation. All the while, gangs of small pirates swarmed
anti-socially over land and water, noisily and violently
re-enacting what appeared to be Swallows and Amazons
and the Driller-Killers go Ape; a petition for the abolition

of life-jackets for the under-tens could have soon gained at least five signatures. But almost more disquieting, and equally dislocated from the Arthur Ransome world of boating, were the adults who occasionally strolled by. For them, a common complaint was the excessive number of French in France — though the likelihood that ABTA would provide a refund on these grounds appeared remote. In consequence, the flooding of the Yonne, a flagrant breach of the holiday agreement, seemed to be regarded by them not as a freak of nature, but as somehow conclusive proof of the historic unreliability of the French character. This off their chest, the disturbingly unconventional design of French toilets — the British bourgeoisie's definitive test of civilisation — would usually surface next, and with it a music-hall dissertation on con-tinental hygiene. For some, their protracted stay in Clamecy was dominated by a constant study of Europe's exchange rate — being shrewd business-like tourists, they were concerned lest they had not invested in a competitively cost-effective culture. For others, with imported tea-bags running low, the crisis was cuisine, and they clearly regarded confinement in a provincial French town as the cause of dietary privation on a scale not suffered since the siege of Leningrad. As the day wore away, all that the scene seemed to lack was visiting football hooligans.

In the sober light of the next morning, the options were no longer complicated. We decided to turn *Beaujolais* round — in one of the 97-point turns that had made our navigation famous the length of the canal — and retrace our wash the few nautical miles to our last resting-point, and then hole up nearby for the next 24 hours. Encouragingly, there was now on board a fragile harmony of spirit, although the short much-abused life of the two alternative suggestions (my proposal for an excursion to a cathedral, and Trixie's proposal for a visit to the circus) did not yet indicate a full unanimity of mind.

The dense fresh green of the early morning woodland was an invigorating sight as we respooled our way temporarily South, but accompanying our navigational *volte-face* was a new and nagging cause of unease. Best labelled as 'etiquette', it grew steadily more tangible as our changed schedule brought the last lock of yesterday into view as the first lock of today. It was the predicament of the non-tipper.

The general social rule on tipping in France is to tip all those who provide good service . . . and all those who provide bad service . . . and all those who don't provide any service whatsoever. And, just to be on the safe side, everyone else within sight, including passing strangers. But lock-keepers seemed to be a grey area. We had no desire to be mean, especially as the majority helped us muddle through with a warm leathery grin and a convivial lockside chat − but we could never decide whether this was highly professional rustic PR, from the cross-my-palm-with-silver charm-school, or traditional rural hospitality, from sensitive souls liable to be instantly mortified by the merest clink of a loose centime. The consequence was guilt and a barge burdened with a fridgeful of pet goats' cheeses and enough fresh vegetables to bring relief to an average-sized town; instead of dispensing one-franc gratuities, we had come to operate like a floating EEC intervention fund, buying up all available lock-keepers' surpluses and putting them into store.

All the same, in the eyes of the lock-keeping world (not all of whom were also goat-keeping greengrocers), we were still non-tippers and the first rule for a non-tipper is to never visit the same place twice. Unfortunately, not only was our holiday voyage inevitably a return trip, but now the next few locks would see our shambling non-paying presence four times in all, and we felt rather like children pressing a traffic lights button for devilment.

And we were apprehensive. In Paris, misjudgements over *le service* can have legendary consequences: the blinding torch in the eye from the enraged usherette, the boiling coffee in the groin by the spurned waiter. In deepest Burgundy, therefore, when faced with the frenzied whirl-pool of the first lock of the day, we had more than a passing worry as to how many non-tippers made it safely back to base.

At this first lock, however, we were greeted as old friends — or at least as the largest bulk-buyers of goat-cheese in the history of the canal. We were even shown a bird's nest in the cottage's wooden letter-box, and told the slang for someone with a broken arm — though told it with such laughter that one suspected a double meaning. The keeper was a stubbled man in his fifties, an apparent bachelor, and he moved at the pace of canal-water. To-gether we all leaned on his old pack-horse bridge in the sunlight, and he told us toothless anecdotes about his life — not one word of which survived the twin problems of language and gums. Yet by the time the water-levels had equalized, we too had established a certain rapport. We warned him we would soon be back, and he waved us cheerfully off.

But our apprehensions were not, alas, unfounded, and a lock or two further on our reception fell definitely short of the Tourist Board's recommended norms.

Occasionally on the canal one would come across ageing male lock-keepers who appeared to be practising neo-Trappists, and who would greet one's arrival with a vow of surly silence that not even the classic code-words '*M'sieurdame*' could crack. This disconcerting hostility was usually the evidence that the keeper was an *invalide de guerre* who had been given the post many years ago as a sinecure. (The French always regard their war-wounded as covered with *la gloire* and place them in privileged positions, unlike the English who see them

126

as military cock-ups and hide them in cupboards; in France there is even a hierarchy of the disabled, and a man who has lost his leg by mismanagement is expected to surrender his seat to a man who has had it blown off by a shell.) Because of the Canal du Nivernais's ancient origins, it was built to a width that precludes commercial traffic, and therefore, as the old soldiers had accepted their post and their cottage and their rocking-chair in the bygone days of a pre-tourist era, they had, not unreasonably, expected never to set eyes on a boat in their lifetime. But, since the Seventies, leisure had burst upon the world, and now each year, their retirement sinecures gave them control of more boats than Eisenhower had had on D-Day. As this had provided the veterans with the relaxed sedentary life-style of a yo-yo, various among them had, in retaliation, developed a welcome of impenetrable silence, perfected to Fifth Amendment proportions. Such was its implicit reproach that one felt like a rambler claiming right-of-way through a bedroom.

We remembered him from the outward journey: a tall khaki figure, with braces and black Army surplus boots, he was gaunt and unbending, though whether from discipline or hidden invalidity was hard to determine. This time, the gates ahead were against us, and so, as Susan nuzzled the boat into the bank and the others made fast, Trixie and I and a pack of Gitanes went on in front to make our presence known. He was on the lockside, looking away from us up-canal, when we tried our first *'Bonjour!'*. A minute flicker of an eyelid, in all probability a tic, was his sole response. We then tried *'Quel beau matin!'* and then, after a short pause, followed this with *'Nous avons un bateau!'* in conjunction with the offer of a cigarette. But apart from a subliminal glance at our shorts, and a possible hardening of distaste around the mouth, there was no discernible reaction, or, indeed, visible sign of life. Uncertain what to do next, but determinedly resisting Trixie's stage-whispered 'Why don't you tap his knee?', I was about to try *'J'aime beaucoup le Burgundy'*, when I heard the distant sound of a dance-band.

Following the man's military gaze, we saw a small private cruiser come into view — this, we guessed correctly, was the cause of our delay. We watched it approach with interest, as the rare sight of another boat in a lock promised to be educational.

It was indeed educational — for all of us. Mounted on the boat were loudspeakers, which continuously broadcast upbeat holiday rhythms, at anti-social decibels. On board were two middle-aged men and a young woman. The man at the helm, in unashamed peaked cap, had marginally the smaller beer-gut, and would occasionally release the wheel to prance around the bridge with castanets. The second man, whose stomach flesh hung loosely over unflattering knee-length bleached jeans, was jiving datedly and unconvincingly on the aft-deck, his blonde partner in pink shorts wearing an expression of ill-concealed boredom. A home-movie camera was fixed to the bow of the boat, filming the passing scenery. As the *ménage* came within earshot, the man at the helm twitched ecstatically and burst with grossly affected *joie de vivre* into atrocious song — the lyrics of which betrayed an unmistakable Germanness, and immediately caused the features of our *invalide de guerre* to give a most unecstatic twitch of their own.

Then the singer-helmsman, posturing as if in a trance, brought the boat slowly and uneasily alongside the bollards, the speakers blaring out musical happiness. Grinning unceasingly, and gesturing at the blue sky, he called out to us, *'C'est la vie, c'est ça, à peu près?'*, to which there was no answer — especially as he was wearing headphones. The ropes were thrown ashore. The lock-keeper pointedly ignored them, and moved towards the open lock-gates. The rather tired-looking, and once good-looking, woman jumped off the boat to make them fast, leaving the two males still gyrating hiply to the echoing sounds. 'I think,' said Trixie, 'it's Rock Around The Lock time!'

The lock-keeper ratcheted the gates with controlled disgust, ignoring, his face like granite, all entreaties to move with the music. They offered him a can of German lager. He marched, eyes front, back along the lock, to wait alone beside the far gates. As he stood staring along the canal, the cine-camera was detached from its stand, and the scene and his posture were filmed from all angles. While the water emptied slowly out, the brick walls of his lock filled up with cheap bebop. The instant that the water-levels became equal, he thrust against the lock controls and icily manhandled the gates open. Then he contemptuously turned his gaunt back upon the cheers and wolf-whistles and, as the boat and the beat eased out into the canal, he carefully and vigorously spat into the water eight feet below.

Trixie and I exchanged looks. For once we were agreed. Neither of us had the stomach for disturbing him three times in as many days whilst we pottered frivolously to and fro along the canal. He possessed a potential for wrath that could turn fickle, feckless holidaymakers like ourselves into the nautical equivalent of pillars of salt. The scene had also, as at Clamecy, made us feel the very act of tourism to be a tacky and dishonourable practice. So we left the khaki figure, louring silently outside his cottage door, and returned to sell a Plan B to the others.

We reached *Beaujolais Deux* at the same time as the floating juke box. We watched it pass our moorings with much noise and synthetic bonhomie, and waited for it to draw ahead before seeking out a suitable spot to tie up for the day. As their cruiser moved on down the canal, we saw them re-attach the camera, this time pointing it deckwards. Then, as the dance-band played on, the young woman removed her pink shorts, along with all else, and – carefully positioning herself for the lens – she mounted the prone form of the larger-gutted of the two, whilst the singing helmsman continued to shake his castanets and view the proceedings from above.

CHAPTER FIFTEEN

Thwarted yet again in our holiday plans, we chose some shade for our moorings, and tied up under overhanging trees. We also chose the bank with the towpath, lest we grounded again and needed the assistance of an able-bodied village. There was, however, not a village in sight. Our reluctance to go South and our inability to go North had resulted in a distinct shortage of available canal. Like most unmetaphorical backwaters, though, it was not short of life: for company, we soon had a family of goslings, as visitors from the nearby woods, a pair of red squirrels, and as entertainment in the reeds opposite, something furry and wet. In fact, it was a lovely spot, but it was also a lovely day and gradually a consensus emerged for the inauguration of the bicycles.

It was a rare and surprising unanimity. Arabella was in favour because she suspected bicycling might be a radical activity; Angus was in favour because, I think, he had decided that physical action could improve his image problem; Susan's enthusiasm was more puzzling

— possibly, after ferry-sickness, car-sickness and barge-sickness, she had come to regard a holiday as primarily an opportunity to be ill in fresh surroundings; and I . . . well, I regarded it as a chance to surreptitiously tick off some items in my Michelin — I had managed to compile, though discreetly, a short check-list of the more interesting socio-historico-architecturalo sights in the immediate vicinity (an example of what Trixie called my cultural Bingo cards) which I felt the well-informed barge-crew of today should be *au fait* with. Trixie herself, having only one handlebar-holder, was *hors de bicyclette*, but proved more than happy to stay on her own and listen once more to the lapping of the water in her gin.

Indeed, the only reservations about going for a ride appeared to come from the bicycles themselves. A week of sleeping rough on deck, exposed to the more unpleasant elements of life, had left them stiff, discoloured, suffering trouble with their joints, and generally short on air; the life of a rent-bike is usually nasty, brutish and short, and they clearly lacked enthusiasm for sight-seeing. And so, before we could start, it was all hands to the pumps and spanners. But a bike is less of a mystery of the universe than a boat, and with a twist and a turn and a rub and a blow, each of them was soon as good as second-hand. Then, after a few recapping wobbles around the deck, and a bit of jockeying for possession, the four of us were off and riding.

At first, we were an ad-man's dream. Fresh-faced young couples, hair flowing, tan glowing, cycling through dappled sunlight, beside dimpled water, by verdant pastures, any onlooker would have unhesitatingly thought we were advertising country butter. And cycling along the towpath, warm wind in our hair, did indeed have an exhilarating, almost liberating effect. The towpath was unmade: it was not so much the open road, more the open rut; sometimes grass, sometimes mud, sometimes puddle, sometimes fallen tree, but nearly always fun . . . except possibly for the bicycles.

After a few miles, we reached a canal bridge and we turned onto a proper road, with its pot-holes provided by a council. By now it was definitely warmer. The bicycles were miniature models, not a size our bodies came in, and they seemed to require the sort of effort usually found in Jane Fonda work-out books. It was an energy at odds with the serenity of our surroundings. The English celebrate and immortalize an Arcadian landscape, full of ducks and geese and hens and goats, which is now mostly gone, but to one's lasting gratitude it is alive and well and sleeping in rural France. The old-world farm-yards that we pedalled past would have held few surprises for Constable; the little orchards that we puffed past still grew in random patterns that would shock agribusiness; and the village pumps that we stopped at still delivered cool water with the force of a Mentholated mountain stream. And against these ancient and harmonious back-drops, the sight of us sweating through on our modern metal child-size pedal-cycles, all of matching make and colour (and clearly a tourist job-lot), lacked, we began to feel, a certain dignity.

Dignity was not much helped by the increasing failure of our makeshift repairs. No amount of latter-day scenery could distract from the fact that there was not a buttock yet built which could exercise control of my saddle, that Angus's chain appeared to have achieved perpetual motion (a discovery for which he displayed unexpectedly little scientific enthusiasm), and that each of Arabella's pedals was as loose as Susan's handlebars, whose fav-ourite position suggested they wanted to go home (as indeed, with growing frequency, did she). By the time we had halted to mend a third puncture, it was becoming clear that our memories of childhood and bicycles had been seen through rose-coloured rear-view mirrors.

We were *en* approximate *route* for Metz-le-Comte (I was keen – in a carefully laid-back way – that we should see a 12th century church set among lime trees with a strange flat roof and now the only remains of the stronghold of the Comtes de Nevers and having a fine view) but the exact whereabouts of each village in which we broke down was increasingly a mystery – although I had an itinerary in mind, I had no map in pocket, as I had come to feel the sin of organisation was best concealed. Consequently the appearance of road junctions now began to sow the first seeds of tension. (The intellectual strength of the French being in abstract thought, they have never fully mastered the physical precision required for a successful signpost.) But we continued to press slowly onwards, through an empty drowsing world where placid village ponds offered the only sanctuary from the growing heat of the hottest afternoon of the holiday so far.

The second seeds of tension were sown by the appearance of fundamental design flaws in the bikes' structures. Whilst we had not hired folding bicycles, we started to find ourselves in possession of collapsing bicycles. ('Folding' is controlled by the owner, 'collapsing' is controlled by the bicycle; the former occurs after a journey, the latter occurs while still on the move.) As a lengthening list of desirable items (nuts, bolts, screws, spokes) made bids for independence, it grew ever plainer that the only experience relevant to riding the bikes was seven years' experience at Billy Smarts'.

Meanwhile, the true significance of Metz-le-Comte was beginning to dawn. The key word was 'view', or, in the original French, '*un large panorama*'. Panoramas are rarely found at sea-level. Indeed, almost without exception, their preference is for the tops of very large hills. And, the further we moved out of the river-valleys, the more we found ourselves faced with these aforementioned hills. This was undeniably a set-back. The hills were not only too steep to ride up, because the pedals were slipping, but also too steep to ride down, because the brakes were missing.

We started to do our cycling on foot. Carrying an increasingly large collection of spare bicycle parts.

With our bicycles disintegrating into their basic components, our group started to follow suit. At each contentious cross-roads, there were as many proposals as there were roads available. Few proposals concerned Metz-le-Comte. Angus was usually keen to find an air-conditioned *bibliotèque*, Susan to find a qualified chemist, and Arabella to discover a lawyer who could advise her on French consumer laws. Inevitably, and familiarly, the arguments began to focus less and less on geography, more and more on personality.

For a short while, we did continue to climb, but so too did the temperature. There was no respite. The trees grew fewer, the shade grew less, the sun grew higher. We all grew slower. And then, in a climactic climatic holiday first, the tarmac started to melt.

I tried to plug the charm and beauty of our destination, but it was fast becoming a lost viewpoint. And, unlike on a canal boat, every single member of a bicycle-crew has freedom of action. And so, one by one, as the going got stickier, every single member pushed off in a huff and a sweat. What had begun as a carefree group outing, albeit apparently from the Ministry of Silly Cycles, ended up as four quite separate and bizarrely-overloaded walkers wandering aimlessly through the countryside looking like a lost back-up team from the Tour de France.

Even *I* never reached Metz-le-Comte. Eventually, I too had to turn around, and it became another Auxerre, another unattainable goal, another cultural victim of the forces of nature. Another holiday cock-up.

After some miles of wandering vaguely valleywards,

I came across another of those endlessly long, straight French roads, which enable the population to test their cars to destruction. It was the kind of road which makes all progress seem an optical illusion. At the end of it, I found myself in a village square, where a certain post-siesta life was detectable, and so I settled down in its one pavement cafe and ordered a much-needed *citron pressé*. And prepared to watch the world go by.

There is nothing that can be added to the extensive literature on the pleasure of sitting in French pavement cafes and watching the world go by. Except for what happened next.

In the square were the usual folkloric clichés: the grizzled old peasant, the grey-blue *deux chevaux* van of 1840, the widow in black carrying a *baguette*, and a couple of aimless young scooter-revvers. On the crumbling brick wall above the *boulangerie* opposite, still visible in huge fading black letters was painted the pre-war command '*Exigez Le Brilliantine!*' Flyposted near the *mairie* was forgotten layer upon forgotten layer of flyblown political agitation, degenerating slowly into dust. Oh, and somewhere a cock crowed. It was the atmosphere that enables every visiting Francophile to assert that little ever changes.

Suddenly a ghetto-blaster filled the square. Military music drowned all other sound. I waited for the dance section of the riot police to arrive. But the noise came from the 19th century school playground to my right. And onto the playground came a brisk school-mistress in her thirties, followed by rows and rows of ten year-old drum majorettes. With a goose-stepping precision usually only seen in Goldenbowl, they lined up in sub-thigh gymslips, and then, twirling their pikestaffs in a precocious unison, they marched up and down the playground for the duration of two *citrons pressés* — all the time with a Yankee gusto that suggested their genes had dual nationality. I watched entranced and appalled. No-one else took any notice. And then they all marched out of sight again. And the ghetto-blaster was silenced. It was not the France of my brochures. And I suspected that if the noise had reached to Colombey-les-deux-Eglises (which seemed acoustically possible) a well-known 6'4'' president would be turning in his patriotic grave.

I have no explanation. My French was not up to explanations. All I knew was that the holiday was just not going to plan. I paid my bill and I and my hot bike-pieces set off once more, in the rumoured direction of the canal.

* * *

Back aboard, the scene was surprisingly tranquil. Regrettably, this was not due to harmony, but the fact that upon their straggling return, each person had immediately retreated to their own cabin; had it been a barge with room service we might never have met again. Such monasticism was not, however, altogether caused by personal animosities. It was also a feeling that death is a private matter.

Between them, the sun and the bicycles had divided up each body into separate regions for chastisement. Territorially speaking, the bicycles had gone for the hands, the wrists, the ankles, the calves, the inner thighs and the buttocks; the sun had sovereignty over the faces, the necks, the arms, the backs of the knees, and all exposed torsos. Like old school maps, our bicycle areas were marked in black and blue, our sun areas in salmon-pink, going on red. Not a lot was left uncoloured. As a result, below-deck echoed pitifully to all the moans and groans and whimpers of a slave-ship that was late for delivery. Indeed, given our general condition, there is probably an internationally-recognised flag we could have flown, instructing every vessel in the vicinity to proceed at once with all available embrocation.

Nonetheless, the impression should not be given that, had we been feeling better, we would have been speaking to each other. After this latest day's travails, a feeling was firmly taking hold that as a group we were constitutionally incapable of co-existing on land *or* water. At some moments, even the thought of playing a non-league game of noughts and crosses appeared fraught with hidden conflict and violence. Indeed, in such a frame of mind, the extra burdens of disabling pain and disfiguring blotches felt somehow complementary to the agony and the angst of the holiday so far. As we ached away feverishly in semi-solitary, it began to seem that the only meaning to it all had to be religious: perhaps our holiday was secretly run by Job Tours (OT) Ltd., and after the flood and the heatwave would come the plague of frogs. Whatever the cause, the estrangements were taking on an air of permanence, and, as afternoon went and evening came, the boat remained silent and apparently deserted.

It was the drainage system that brought us back together. So widespread were the demands on the leaking shower-unit that the rising water-level in the adjoining cabins aft resulted in three urgent applications for refugee status. And so, with the dirty shower-water dribbling its way through our cast-off clothing like an incoming tide of used froth, we reluctantly made our way for'ard.

Together once more in the State Room, the gathering had somewhat the stilted air of a cocktail party. This, though, was due not so much to emotional sensitivity as to the fact that we all felt physically unable to sit down or, indeed, place any part of our bodies in any proximity to anything. Even our stomachs had to make do with a *vin rouge* and some pensionable Stilton, so tender were the cooking limbs. Not surprisingly, self-pity was the main order of the day.

Even so, our traumas were for a moment unexpectedly quite forgotten when we suddenly found ourselves witness to the aesthetic climax of the week: a glorious, full-blooded sunset. We had fortuitously tucked the boat in an ideal position to watch the dying light stream through the overhanging foliage. As it tinged the canal a fading scarlet, the last of the baby ducks scuttled for bed; as it touched the horizon, the cattle in the meadows cast shadows the length of giraffs in the veldt; as the banks fell into darkness, the ripples of unseen rising fish glistened into view . . . Almost a perfect end to an imperfect day.

Almost.

It was a simple enough desire: a breath of alcohol-free evening air and the timeless sounds of *la campagne* at night. Somewhere a porthole was opened. A breeze stirred a curtain. And ten thousand mosquitoes dropped in for a nightcap of blood.

CHAPTER SIXTEEN

Next morning, we were under way almost before the lock-keepers were ready with their ratchets.

It was a promptness born less of enthusiasm than insomnia. Winks of sleep had been few and far between. Burnt, bruised and bitten is a rare combination of afflictions; and to feel eight pints of blood short *and* worried about malaria can make sleep difficult.

It was another lovely morning. The passing scenery was now quite familiar. Even the lock-keepers' goats were starting to recognise us. The days of heatwave had virtually mopped up the field-size puddles, and normal service had been resumed again in the countryside. All around dragonflies and damselflies were back on their flight-paths, safe at last from bullet-force rain. And on the towpath, there was even a seigneurial rider, complete with black hunting dog, out for his constitutional canter.

Little of this was widely observed, for I was alone on deck. Below, luggage was being transferred between fore and aft cabins. It was being done with acrimony. Initially

140

a subtle ploy of mine to gain control of the engine at the end of Week One, it had backfired last night; at the exact moment when the entire State Room had been filled with the massed whine of mosquitoes on bombing runs, Arabella had announced herself ready for the change-over. However, even Susan and I knew that possession is nine-tenths of the law and had immediately retreated aft, leaving her and Angus to spend the night doing a commendable impression of St. Vitus's dancers. They had not been best pleased.

Back up on deck, as *Beaujolais Deux* passed yet another apple orchard mysteriously free of France's dreaded Golden Delicious, thus giving credence to the view that they are made in soap factories, I started to contemplate the prospects for Week Two. Despite everything, despite ourselves even, we were developing a proficiency with locks, and with proficiency Clamecy was only a day from Corbigny. This would leave us three days to press onward. And in just a mile or so the strait-jacket of the canal would for the first time give way to the liberty-bodice of the river. We could, I calculated, still end up within a taxi-fare of elusive Auxerre.

A friendly shout came from a familiar stubbled face ahead. The gates were in our favour and, easing in, I made the gentlest of contacts with his lock. As we waited for the levels to draw equal, I noticed that the same dead fish from the day before was still rising and falling with the lock water. The gates opened, and the keeper wished us '*Bonne chance!*'. I waved goodbye.

His was the last lock before Clamecy. Everyone stayed on deck now, but, for medical reasons, they remained in the cockpit which was still shaded from the sun. On the final lap, the bow wave seemed even slower than before. This time, though, it was not just impatience, but familiarity as well; there was an understandable sense of *déjà vu* as we clocked up the last mile.

This sense was dramatically increased as we came around the last, long curve into town — and heard the same roar as before, only louder, and saw the same traffic jam as before, only longer. And met the same English tourists as before, only crosser.

Enquiry taught us two facts. From our compatriots, we gathered that, could they but master the French telephone system, we would witness the world's first consular airlift of emergency baked beans and cornflakes. From the lady of the lock, we learnt that our lowland storm had become someone else's upland storm, and that high in the mountains the equivalent of a reservoir bath-plug had been pulled — and that enough bathwater for the whole of France was now on its way to the sea. Through Clamecy.

In retrospect, there was remarkably little discussion. The boat was moored. A show of hands was called for. Angus was volunteered to go to the train station. And the rest of us awaited his return with the Renault.

The canal, it was agreed, should be explored by car. Among our possible destinations would be Auxerre, engine and quorum willing.

Arabella was particularly fulsome about this solution.

'But,' I said, unable to resist, 'cars are so anti-social, so damaging to the environment.'

From the look I received in reply, I could already tell it was not going to be a peaceful second week.

THE END

A SELECTED LIST OF HUMOUR TITLES AVAILABLE FROM CORGI BOOKS

THE PRICES SHOWN BELOW WERE CORRECT AT THE TIME OF GOING TO PRESS. HOWEVER TRANSWORLD PUBLISHERS RESERVE THE RIGHT TO SHOW NEW RETAIL PRICES ON COVERS WHICH MAY DIFFER FROM THOSE PREVIOUSLY ADVERTISED IN THE TEXT OR ELSEWHERE.

☐ 13317 5	**PRIVATE PARTS**	*Russell Ash & Bernard Higton*	£2.95
☐ 13318 3	**I'LL DRINK TO THAT**	*Russell Ash & Bernard Higton*	£2.95
☐ 13319 1	**THEY DON'T REALLY MEAN IT**		
		Russell Ash & Bernard Higton	£2.95
☐ 11525 8	**CLASS**	*Jilly Cooper*	£2.95
☐ 17463 0	**FATHERHOOD**	*Bill Cosby*	£2.50
☐ 99301 8	**THE WHOLE HOG**	*Oliver Dalton & Gray Jolliffe*	£3.95
☐ 99312 3	**CATMOPOLITAN**	*Irene Hochberg*	£5.95
☐ 99137 6	**GRAFFITI 6**	*Roger Kilroy*	£1.50
☐ 99045 0	**GRAFFITI 5: AS THE ACTRESS SAID TO THE BISHOP**	*Roger Kilroy*	£1.75
☐ 99022 1	**GRAFFITI 4**	*Roger Kilroy*	£1.50
☐ 11812 5	**GRAFFITI 3**	*Roger Kilroy*	£1.50
☐ 98116 8	**GRAFFITI 2**	*Roger Kilroy*	£1.50
☐ 98079 X	**GRAFFITI: THE SCRAWL OF THE WILD**	*Roger Kilroy*	£1.75
☐ 12865 1	**LOVE FORTY**	*Sue Limb*	£2.95
☐ 12796 5	**ONE MAN AND HIS BOG**	*Barry Pilton*	£1.95
☐ 13233 0	**ONE MAN AND HIS LOG**	*Barry Pilton*	£2.50
☐ 13038 9	**OKKER CHIC**	*Michael Thomas*	£3.95
☐ 13050 8	**BALDIES**	*Berkman Thompson*	£1.50
☐ 99266 6	**THE CAT EMPIRE (Large format)**	*Michael Weigall*	£4.95

All Corgi/Bantam Books are available at your bookshop or newsagent, or can be ordered from the following address:

Corgi/Bantam Books,
Cash Sales Department,
P.O. Box 11, Falmouth, Cornwall TR10 9EN

Please send a cheque or postal order (no currency) and allow 60p for postage and packing for the first book plus 25p for the second book and 15p for each additional book ordered up to a maximum charge of £1.90 in UK.

B.F.P.O. customers please allow 60p for the first book, 25p for the second book plus 15p per copy for the next 7 books, thereafter 9p per book.

Overseas customers, including Eire, please allow £1.25 for postage and packing for the first book, 75p for the second book, and 28p for each subsequent title ordered.